MOON NIBBLER

The Art of Pat Strakowski

MOON NIBBLER
The Art of Pat Strakowski

Andrew Oko / Photography by John W. Heintz

Frontenac House

Published by
Frontenac House Ltd.
1138 Frontenac Avenue S.W.
Calgary, Alberta, T2T 1B6, Canada
www.FrontenacHouse.com

Copyright © Andrew Oko, 2009
Printed and bound in Canada
Library and Archives Canada Cataloguing in Publication

Oko, Andrew, 1946-
    Moon nibbler : the art of Pat Strakowski / Andrew
Oko ; photography by John W. Heinz.

Includes index.
ISBN 978-1-897181-28-7

    1. Strakowski, Pat--Criticism and interpretation.
I. Strakowski, Pat II. Heintz, John W. III. Title.

NB249.S85O36 2009   730.92   C2009-903566-9

Book and cover design: Epix Design
Front cover/jacket image: John W. Heintz
Back cover/jacket image: John W. Heintz
Author photo: Neil Petrunia
Photographic sources: pp 78, 79 Glenbow Museum; 105 Greg Clarke; pp 102,103
Whyte Museum of the Canadian Rockies; pp 9,10,14 archival photos in possession of
the artist.

The photographs in this book were taken by John W. Heintz. All photographs, except
for those listed above, remain the property of the publisher and permission must be
gained in writing from Frontenac House to reproduce or use them in any way.

Frontenac House gratefully acknowledges the support of the Canada Council for the
Arts for our publishing program. We also gratefully acknowledge the support of The
Alberta Foundation for the Arts.

Canada Council   Conseil des Arts
for the Arts   du Canada

Alberta
Foundation
for the Arts

Preface

What I value most about the art of Pat Strakowski is the mythic imagination that has led to a body of extraordinary work.

The opportunity to write this book has been a twofold challenge for me. From the moment I first entered Pat's studio I have been entranced by her ideas, which are as varied as they are extensive. Over a period of approximately 30 years, she has produced an impressive range of amazing sculptures; I know from my study of her slide library that the pieces illustrated here represent but a small fraction of her output.

In view of this output, it is perhaps surprising that relatively little has been written of an interpretive, analytical or critical nature about her work. When discussing this project with numerous admirers of her sculpture we often heard comments to the effect of "at last, a book is being written about Pat Strakowski." Thus I understood that my first challenge would be to develop at least an initial understanding of her artistry, of its scope and insight, of its originality of imagination and concept.

The second challenge would be to place her work within the context of mythology in the contemporary world. Of course this study was necessary in furthering my understanding of Pat Strakowski's world view, but inevitably it was personal as well. Pat understood this and was always patient with my questions, often asserting that her art is open to interpretation. I fondly recall our numerous meetings in her studio over the course of a year and a half. During this time she contributed her own personal insights about the various pieces in this publication. Her methods of working, the influences and sources of ideas that affected her art, the concepts that she was embodying in the pieces – all these elements were touched upon in our discussions. About half way through the publication process we hit upon the idea of simply recording her observations and converting the transcripts into a series of sculpture-by-sculpture commentaries of the pieces in the book. This proved easy to do – with little or no editing, the commentaries performed admirably as descriptions both of the pieces themselves and the creative impetus behind them.

As I continued my study of Pat's work I became increasingly aware of the multi-layered subtleties in design and execution that are seldom obvious on first viewing. That of course is not unusual with any examination of works of art, but I did find it interesting that the photographer, John Heintz, experienced similar feelings during his photography sessions. Over and over again he would comment that each time he shot a piece from a different angle, or with different lighting, or in close-up mode rather than from a distance, he would pick up on some detail or feature that he hadn't noticed in earlier photo sessions.

And that may well be the most important point of all – that with Pat Strakowski's sculpture, as with any complex work of art, repeated observation yields ever-expanding insight.

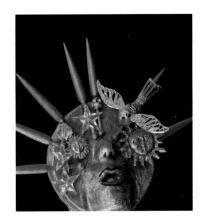

Moon Nibbler
The Art of Pat Strakowski

A vision of the Calgary of Pat Strakowski's childhood is coming to mind. It is a summer evening in the Bridgeland-Riverside district early in the 1940s. To the west the sun is sinking under the mountains with a golden-scarlet glow that ripples the surface of the Bow River on the south with myriad reflections.

The district is nestled in the river valley. A resident is bringing home a cow he had tethered to graze on the hills behind. Many of the residents keep chickens or rabbits, which are now settling down for the night in their backyard coops or pens. Rhubarb and horseradish choke the sides of the back alleys and the backyards are filled to their margins with victory gardens. The streets are dirt and gravel but First Avenue North is paved and many of the sidewalks are concrete, bearing the date 1912, a remnant of the Calgary boom years immediately predating the First World War. It was during this boom period that the General Hospital was built in the area and a streetcar connected the district with the centre of Calgary to the south via the Langevin Bridge, originally built in 1885.[1]

It is a culturally diverse neighbourhood. Bridgeland has a large Italian population, and a German community is prominent in Riverside, but there are also Ukrainian, Russian, Polish, and Asian groups. For many immigrants the district is their first Canadian home, but for others it is a place to stop off before continuing their Canadian journey.

A two-storey brick house stands on the sloping southeast corner of Centre Avenue and Sixth Street Northeast. There are four victory gardens in the backyard. Four families and an elderly widow occupy the premises. Ukrainian immigrants Katarina (née Krupa) and Wasil Dmytrychyn live with their daughter Petrusia in the front of the ground floor. The Drahanchuk family, of Russian origin, lives in the back. The second floor is occupied by the Rogalski family and the Kunch family, who are Polish and German respectively. A Polish widow known as Mrs. Miller lives in the attic.

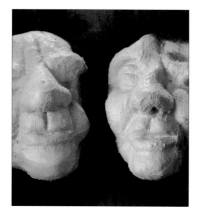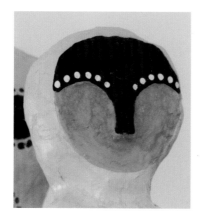

The Dmytrychyns have readied their daughter for bed. Now as Katarina settles to embroider roses on a blouse, Wasil sits besides Petrusia's bed to tell a bedtime story. Pat Strakowski remembers her father as a storyteller, an inherited trait that she asserts is central to her own work but in the visual rather than the verbal realm. The following tale, among her earliest personal recollections, offers a magic stemming from a suspension of disbelief that comes easily for a listening child. However, the adult cultivation and practice of such an imagination requires a commitment to living in an extraordinary world. The magic recalled from childhood now resonates in the work of the mature artist.

"When I was a little boy we were so poor that I didn't have a mother and father so I lived with Babusia and Dido. One day Dido and I mounted our horse and rode to the woods for firewood. Dido had a wood axe in his belt so when we arrived we found that the wood axe had cut the horse in two and the back half was gone. We retraced our steps and found the back half lying there. Dido attached the two ends with a stump and we carried on. When we returned to the forest we noticed that the stump had grown into a mighty oak tree.

"The branches of the tree came all the way to the ground so I climbed the tree. When I got to the top there was a huge nest with three large eggs. I carefully put the eggs into my cap and we took them home. The eggs tasted very good after days of nothing but kasha.

"Every day afterwards I would return to the mighty oak and climb it to the top. And sure enough there were three eggs waiting for me in the nest."

Later, Petrusia grew curious about her family background and the war. Both Katrina Krupa, born in 1909, and Wasil Dmytrychyn, born in 1903, had come from the vicinity of Vola Zaleska, a farming village in Galicia. This part of Galicia is now in southeastern Poland near the border with the Ukraine. Prior to the Great War, Galicia belonged to Austria; it suffered great degradation, initially during the First World War from the forces of Austria-Hungary, Russia, Germany-Austria, and the Bolsheviks; and afterwards through the Red army, the White army, the Allied expeditionary force, the Ukrainian army, and the Polish army. Finally in 1921 with the Treaty of Riga, Poland recognized the Soviet Ukraine and annexed the western Ukraine. This included Galicia, which belonged to Poland between the two world wars.

Katrina emigrated to Canada in 1927. Wasil emigrated about the same time. Their families had known each other in the old country. Katrina and Wassil met again in Calgary in the early thirties and married shortly thereafter. Wasil worked as a riveter for Dominion Bridge, and Katrina as a cleaning lady. Petrusia was born in 1937.

In 1974, Pat Strakowski made a pilgrimage to the homeland of her parents. There the memories of the hardships of war, the ever-shifting borders, and the bitterness associated with ethnic conflicts were not far from the surface of people's minds.

The Dmytrychyn family moved twice within the Bridgeland-Riverside area, each time to a larger rental unit, later purchasing a home in the Mission district south of the Bow River. Pat has recalled that for social occasions she and a friend would gravitate back to

the neighbourhood haunts of their childhood: to the Ukrainian Community Centre in the east downtown and to the centres of other ethnic organizations in Bridgeland-Riverside. In 1957, she married John Strakowski, of a Polish family background. Pat and John have three daughters: Dorothy, Linda and Shirley.

Pat Strakowski and her mother, circa 1940

Dreaming you call to us, and
We form out of the mists of
Exceptional Pass.
Bearing to the point of origin
We anticipate and participate in
This feast of the senses.[2]

Located on a shelf behind the workbench of Strakowski's second-storey Montgomery studio is an outdoors photo of the artist as a child standing with her mother in the Bridgeland-Riverside district of Calgary circa 1940. They are both wearing traditional Ukrainian dresses; the bold colouring and patterning of the outfits is reflected in the clutter of the studio in which her papier-mâché sculptures merge in concord with the multitude of found objects, work of like-minded artists, and folk art from North America, Mexico, East India and Africa.

But as a whole Pat Strakowski's work does not refer to any specific culture or ethnic background. It is more a personal mythology,

a contemporary hybrid formed of a variety of cultural influences ranging from aboriginal and classical mythology to folk tales and the day-to-day experience of life around her. At the same time the work is informed by her training and immersion in the visual arts.

These influences were apparent as early as 1985, when Strakowski included her work *Spirit Guides in their Magic Craft* in the *Myth of Exceptional Pass* exhibition organized by The Whyte Museum of the Canadian Rockies in Banff, Alberta. Although the work deals with the shaman theme she had already begun in the early eighties, it also anticipates the boat series she started later in the decade. In the sculpture, two spirit guides stand in deep communion atop a donut-shaped boat. An ancient lady with hair flowing almost to the ground holds a baton in one hand and gesticulates with the other. A companion leans back against a staff; she is a vestige, a liminal being – that is, an entity positioned at the threshold between "here" and "there", between "absence" and "presence", between "becoming" or "disappearing".

Strakowski also exhibited *Grandmother Walks Softly*, an ancestor-figure piece she had just completed, in the *Myth of Exceptional Pass* show. The figure is made of papier-mâché over a wire-mesh armature and embellished with various materials ranging from leather and fabrics to feathers and acrylic paint. Strakowski's poem of the same title that accompanies the illustration of the sculpture in the exhibition catalogue manifests the mythopoetic nature of both her own work and the *Exceptional Pass* series of exhibitions:

Grandmother Walks Softly

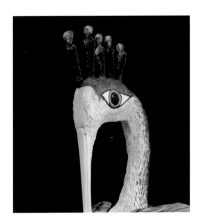

There is a tale grandmothers tell
children, ones who are very young
and still believe.

Of a hidden valley, high in the
mountains, where ice-cold streams
rush past quiet meadows and settle
in deep blue silent lakes.

Of the most magnificent tree living
in this valley, the Great World Tree.
An evergreen whose roots reached
the earth's centre and whose
great trunk rose up past the clouds
to pierce the sky.

Of the time when souls, awaiting
their birth, nested in the branches
of this tree.

This poem then returns to *Spirit Guides in their Magic Craft* to
incorporate that piece into the narrative:

Of the two old spirit guides who
lived on the very tip of the tree in
a magic craft that could sail over
the waves we call the Northern Lights.

Of the great storm that shook the
earth and the great tree trembled
causing the souls to fall

Of the first soul born into a shaman.[3]

Strakowski used a variety of materials to make *Spirit Guides in
their Magic Craft*. She wove the boat with string-bean vines from
her parents' garden and used driftwood detailed with papier-mâché
and painted with acrylic paint to make the figures. Porcupine quills
and gummed silver stars adorn the ancient woman's blue dress. The
woman's hair is made of un-spun wool wrapped here and there with
unbleached linen thread to define the ponytail. From the upper part
of the staff of the vestigial spirit, also wrapped with linen thread, is
suspended a string prickled with porcupine quills that terminates in
red and yellow beads. Next to the woman's baton dangles a string of
miniature silver bells Strakowski found at a Cargo Canada shop that
had materials from all over the world.

Strakowski takes great care in collecting and selecting the objects
and materials she uses, as she puts it, "to embellish" her figures. For
instance, the linen thread used in *Spirit Guides in their Magic Craft*
"is hard to find and has a nice depth to it when it is pulled tight." The
objects that she finds must have a personal resonance: "They have
to talk to you." Her criteria are intuitive. She has repeatedly stated
that the objects she uses must have the feel of artefacts, must "have
a history." The embellishments contribute to the sense of history

in her work. She has collected objects as souvenirs from an early age. Before attending the Alberta College of Art in the late 1970s her preference was for natural rather than manmade objects. At the College, however, where she focused her studies on the subject of textiles, there was much emphasis on recycling materials. She began going to goodwill stores and attending garage sales. She saw many fabrics that were clothes, tablecloths or curtains but only some of these "wanted to be something else." Always she searched for objects such as beads or patterns that could be transformed by putting them into the context of creative work.

This reuse of "found" objects and/or materials or even images in the visual arts, sometimes referred to as "recontextualization", has roots that extend back to the collage and assemblage of Cubism and Dada and the readymades of Marcel Duchamp early in the 20th century. Widespread acceptance was confirmed with the advent of Pop and Conceptual art movements in the 1950s and 60s; and by the late 70s, when Strakowski attended the College, the recycling of everyday objects for creative purposes was already well accepted as a powerful creative tool.

There are many found objects in Strakowski's studio. Prominently situated is a sideboard that her father made. Strakowski has painted the sideboard a golden yellow and the central panel inserts of both the upper and lower pair of doors with representations of the tree of life during the four seasons. As painted, the trees have heavy cylindrical trunks quickly tapering at the top to a canopy of branches. The winter tree has glowing embers deep in its base; the spring tree

has a magpie feeding her young in a nest immediately under the canopy; the summer tree is covered at the trunk with butterflies; the fall tree is filled with rotting vegetation. The doors of the sideboard open to reveal shelves crammed with a colourful collection of statuettes of Christian personalities and other religious kitsch: of Jesus, Mary, various saints, and married couples, standing, enthroned or enshrined. On top of the cabinet are three of Strakowski's papier-mâché skulls. The outside skulls have apple-bearing trees growing out of them. A naked Eve is sitting under the tree on the left; Adam and Eve are entwined in a fiery embrace below the tree on the right. A snake coils around one of its branches. A found statuette of a married couple stands atop the central skull, which is flanked by found statuettes of Mary and a nun on the left and Jesus and a nun on the right. Pat Strakowski is not religious and neither were her parents, so this tableau must be interpreted within the context of her interest in world mythology. It is a thought-provoking assemblage of Christian myth, highly personal and enmeshed with the material culture of the commonplace or popular in the form of the figurines.

In the studio the objects of popular culture have been used in her work or await their reuse in the service of the artist's creative imagination. Reproductions of ancient Greek ceramic ware stand atop a manual pinball machine and inside the open cabinet on which the machine rests. Standing along the base of this machine are glass paperweights of various shapes and designs. A closet with many shelves is jammed with a wide variety of stuffed animals and a variety of metal and plastic toys and figurines.

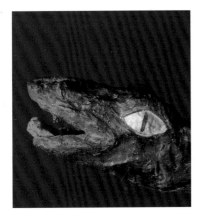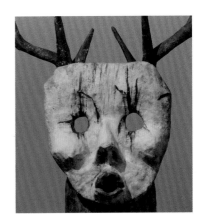

On a trip to New York in 1989, Strakowski visited the retrospective exhibition of pop artist Andy Warhol at the Museum of Modern Art. In the museum shop she acquired a keepsake of the show, a mass-produced brown paper shopping bag with Warhol's full-head three-quarter-view portrait of a cow against an azure sky. This bag hangs in her studio immediately to the left of the sideboard, but suspended over the cow's forehead just above the ears is a white plaster angel with outstretched wings, which she bought at Rubaiyat, a shop in Calgary, because it was a "very folk-art-looking angel." But only when she brought it home did she see a connection between the angel and the bag because the "very friendly cow" with the blue background is "almost angelic itself." To be sure, Warhol himself would have approved of this combination. Such a juxtaposition of disparate objects and images serves to illustrate not only the artist's imagination at work but also the creative potential of considering the union of differing contexts. The importation of "found" objects into art establishes a polarization and the resultant discourse about the mundane world from whence the objects came and the creative or "high" realm of art. This theme is central when considering the issues surrounding Strakowski's work.

In 1979, when Strakowski was in her early forties, she achieved a diploma from the Alberta College of Art with a major in textiles. She had been a secretary at the Southern Alberta Institute of Technology prior to her studies, and became interested in the activities of the College nearby where the exposure to art and artists captured her imagination. She had also attended artist talks and exhibitions, which prompted her to enrol as a student.

In the early 1980s, not long after her graduation from the College, Strakowski was casting about for a direction with her work. The *Exceptional Pass* series of exhibitions at The Whyte Museum of the Canadian Rockies and a course of studies in cultural anthropology that she took at the University of Calgary coincided to fire up her mythic imagination. At this time her artistic practice had focused on weaving and textiles but within a year of beginning her study of cultural anthropology she began making papier-mâché sculptures, a technique she had worked on as a student at the Alberta College of Art. Papier-mâché has a long history of commercial and craft applications beginning in the 17th century in Europe and is thought to be of Asian origin. Strakowski uses a liquid acrylic medium to soak and bind strips of newsprint over armatures that are often made of chicken wire but may also include dowels or folded paper. Surfaces are often covered with gesso, painted and embellished with found objects.

The 1982 exhibition *Exceptional Pass: the Quests, the Expeditions, the Explorations*, the second of the series on Exceptional Pass, clearly struck a responsive chord in the artist, coming as it did at a time when she was particularly interested in learning more about other cultures. Here too, as the first in this series of shows in which she participated, she was confronted with the mythology of place. She submitted two works to this show: *Rock Magician's Pouch* and *Sorcerer's War Oracle*; both were assemblages of objects and materials ranging from feathers, bone, claws, glass, stone, and hair to leather, pigments, and paper.

Rock Magician's Pouch

Sorcerer's War Oracle

It is important to consider the *Exceptional Pass* series of exhibitions because they shed some light on the cultural climate for myth and history in the arts of our time, and consequently Strakowski's enthusiastic response to them.[4] Both visual and literary artists contributed to the mythology for these shows on the theme of a fictive pass in the Canadian Rockies. The creative rationale for the series was to extend interest in the culture and folklore of the Rockies into the development of a sense of place. This was to be a coming-together of artists in a collective, creative act. It was the emotive quality of history that was paramount. A good story was most important in the development of such a history: "If it's not true then it should be true."[5]

The underlying theoretical framework for the *Exceptional Pass* mythology, as developed in the late 1970s, reflected a twofold process: on the one hand the questioning of history and identity common to our postmodern era; and on the other an expression of the desire for cohesive community, for locality in the face of the homogeneity of globalization. Strakowski, as a student at the Alberta College of Art in the late 1970s, and afterwards through being immersed in the art scene, was thoroughly familiar with the askance view of history – history as constructed, invented or imagined as myth. However, in our contemporary world a mythological outlook tends also to promote the notion of fanciful narrative tinged with falseness as far as history or the nature of reality is concerned. How to provide a context for myth today? There is a dilemma of trusting neither history nor mythology that is central to the consideration of

Pat Strakowski's work because it appears to implicate not only an individual's worldview but the signifying function of language itself.

The courses that Strakowski took in cultural anthropology provided new insights on the culture of aboriginal peoples from around the world. The study of rituals and the stories that informed them excited her. One of the courses was on Canadian native art and culture. In 1983, towards the end of the course, Strakowski submitted the work *Spirit Guide* for an assignment dealing with the relationship between the native peoples of the Northwest coast and their materials. *Spirit Guide* is a two-headed figure relating to the out-of-body experience of a shaman's séance. This is a process that has long attracted the interest of cultural anthropologists; Aldona Jonaitis, for instance, in the *Art of the Northern Tlingit*, describes how this magical ritual serves to oppose the normalcy of the profane or secular world to that of the sacred, which is the source of the shaman's power:

> He donned his special costume, shook a variety of percussive instruments that only appeared at such moments, contorted his body, and, finally entered into a trancelike state. Such performances and activities were crucial to the shaman's success, since they symbolically defined and separated the magical arena from the normal world. Sacredness and supernatural power are not absolutes, but instead, can increase or decrease depending upon how far away or close to secularity one

is; when the shaman became distinct from his social world during a séance, he became more sacred, and thus, had more power with which he could succeed in his responsibilities.[6]

A shaman used such ritual for the good of the community in his extensive practice that included healing the sick, controlling the weather, driving out evil spirits, furthering success in hunting and fishing, and warfare. Jonaitis has described the séance as an exchange between the secular and sacred realms, which has three phases: separation, liminality, and incorporation. The separation phase was a process of easing out of the profane realm, when the shaman "removed his normal everyday clothes and donned his distinctive and different shamanic costume, replete with necklaces, charms, and musical instruments."[7] The liminality phase was one of transformation during which the shaman's personality was altered into that of one of his spirit helpers, animals that inhabited the supernatural realm and had been acquired during his initiation through a vision quest. At this level "the spirits gave the shaman their tongues, while the shaman gave the spirits himself."[8] In the final reincorporation phase the paraphernalia that the shaman used refer symbolically "not only to the shaman's own return to the orderly realm of human society, but also functioned to reintegrate his patient into that orderly realm."[9]

In *Spirit Guide* the second head is a manifestation of the shaman's altered state. The figure wears a dancing apron – essential to the shamanic ritual – that is fashioned from fringed deer skin and adorned with a variety of beads and buttons, earrings, skulls, and small, round brass bells. A rosette cut from a pillow case is fastened to the shoulder. The headgear is made of fur taken from a discarded coat. Also essential are the auditory aspects of the shamanic ritual; these are represented by attaching salmon-can lids, shaped to simulate the beaks of puffins, one of the Northwest coast shamanic animals. The puffin beaks would clank together as the shaman danced.

Spirit Guide, however, is not a copy, nor is it similar to any specific Northwest coast Indian work of art. Strakowski was enthralled by the magical quality of the shamanic tradition, and has over the years continued to create works on the theme. One example is the haunting *The Sentinel* of 2001. A supernatural sentinel, the figure has a cylindrical body with no arms; the head is a partially opened eagle's beak. The figure is made of unpainted papier-mâché of a very light orangey colour showing the fine cracklature of the layered paper. Despite the beak, the head is eerily human, with prominent eyebrows over glass eyes. The majestic quality of the figure is enhanced by two horizontal black velvet bands over the chest, each filled with a single row of Chinese coins with small holes in the centre.

Strakowski is aware that the shamanic tradition is universal in scope. When asked about possible criticism that her work may imitate aboriginal traditions in either subject or use of materials, she refers to the ancient practices that once influenced her own culture west of the Urals. She is as much influenced by the appearance of ethnographic art as by its content. And while some of the materials she uses in her work such as hide, bone or feather may indeed

resemble those of aboriginal works, the use of other materials from our own day-to-day world demonstrates that the natural substances are also "found". Indeed, the found objects with which she embellishes her pieces serve at times to disrupt the mythical or magical aura of her work, and instead lead to a questioning of the role of such magic or myth in our contemporary world. The gummed silver stars on the spirit guide's dress in *Spirit Guides in their Magic Craft* or the Chinese coins on the chest bands on the body of *The Sentinel*, for instance, are an example of this disjuncture. The manufactured puffin beaks or the miniature skull on the apron of *Spirit Guide* – perhaps recalling a prize the artist found as a child within a Cracker Jack box – are reminders of the role of popular culture in determining our mythology.

The mythology of non-historical or non-literate cultures from around the world has influenced Strakowski's work, and she understands shamanism as a universal phenomenon within such cultures. Because of her global view, however, such influences are manifest in a general rather than a specific way. Attention is turned instead to contemplating the subjects of ritual and magic as catalysts for the artist's own creative imagination, which in turn leads to a consideration of the relevance of myth in contemporary life.

Strakowski's first sustained body of work utilizing her newly chosen medium of papier-mâché was the Ancestor Series, works that are sequentially numbered according to their order of completion. Typical of the series is *Ancestor 12* of 1982. A haunting figure with a lean, angular face, the gold-brown skin is enhanced by the violet turban with violet, blue and orange stripes that wraps around the head and long neck. Only the slipper-toes of the figure protrude beneath the heavy, square-shaped turquoise robe – the arms are concealed beneath the padded shoulders of the garment. The neck and the slit in the robe beneath the neck are beaded in light blue. Across the chest there are rows of buttons beneath which hang 13 braids of earth-coloured green and orange fabric set off at one end by the light-blue beads and colourful bands and at the other end by more light-blue beads. A prominent chin jutting out above the long neck and flared nostrils lends the ancestor a resolute demeanour. Although the eyes are closed, the right eye bulges out in its socket as if fully aware and all-seeing.

It was with this series of ancestor sculptures that Strakowski came fully to terms with the ritualistic use of her found objects in the embellishment of her works: "I used up all my good stuff on them." The wide array of colourful outfits of these figures conveys an ancestral influence that is diverse and engaging. Although Strakowski's interest in the theme undoubtedly was stimulated by her studies in cultural anthropology – the ancestral past, especially through inherited stories, being of great spiritual importance to aboriginal cultures – most certainly it was her childhood experiences in a multi-cultural neighbourhood that provided the genesis for the theme. Ancestors may be regarded as symbolic agents that serve to root us in this world by establishing our identity and connoting a sense of place. This is a theme frequently developed in literature. Margaret Laurence, for example, has repeatedly examined her

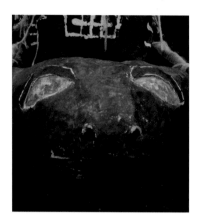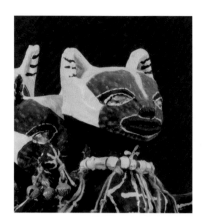

own hometown roots and her relationship to them to indicate the importance of ancestors in determining locality:

> This is where my world began. A world which includes the ancestors – both my own and other people's ancestors who became mine. A world which formed me, and continues to do so, even though I fought it in some aspects, and continue to do so. A world which gave me my own lifework to do, because it was here that I learned the sight of my own particular eyes.[10]

And the work resulting from the sight of Strakowski's eyes, derived from a diverse ethnic background, is her visual legacy.

A series of works on the theme of boats followed the *Spirit Guides in their Magic Craft* of 1985. One of these was *The Incredible Return of the Spirit Clans Down the Mystical Waters of Exceptional Pass in their Magnificent Canoe* of 1991, which was shown in *Return to Exceptional Pass* of 1992, the last of the series of *Exceptional Pass* shows at The Whyte Museum of the Canadian Rockies. The mosquito actively perched at the prow of the boat is followed by several shamanic animals: coyote, yeti, deer, bear, cat, beaver and finally a raven in the stern. Brightly painted in a colour scheme that ranges from rusts, oranges and browns to blues, yellows and whites, they are on their way to a potlatch, a ceremonial feast for the exchange of gifts. The boat itself has painted eyes at the bow and stern as if it were an animate being. The piercing blue eyes of

the mosquito – worry beads from Greece – are an effective contrast to its orangey body. Except for the mosquito and raven, the animals are clutching bundles containing ritualistic charms; for instance, the coyote's bundle is a stick with turquoise beads and leather thongs.

As with myths in general, there are variations on stories of the origins of the mosquito. The version Strakowski remembers involves a group of young hunters who discover a cave in the woods. Inside they find the belongings of the inhabitant of the cave: furs, utensils, foodstuffs. They are about to take these things home when the inhabitant of the cave, an old woman, returns and tells the men that they were her possessions. The men are arrogant and insist they are entitled to the goods because they had found them. In the ensuing argument the men tie the woman to a log and light a fire under her. The woman curses them: "Because you have treated me badly and have no respect for me, this is the curse that I put on you and your kind." The men respond by laughing with derision. But when the fire died down and the charred remains collapsed into the fire, instead of sparks it was mosquitoes that flew out into the world.

At times Strakowski uses the boat motif as a personification of experience. *The Logical Nature of Any Voyage Is Determined by the Limits of Interpretation to their Logical Outcome from the Point of Uncertainty*, completed in 1998, recalls instances of individuals of a group wanting to go in separate directions, like at times a family on vacation. At the prow of the boat is a golden ball. The animated heads and beaks of the birds in the boat convey the clamour of preparation and excitement of anticipation. Each of the birds carries a bundle of

charms to help it for the voyage into the unknown. The sun at the stern appears to be molten in its energy, as if the voyage will know no end. The sun – personified in classical mythology by Helios, who every day drove his chariot across the sky – is wearing earrings and metal feathers that Strakowski found in a bead store. The birds have clearly been inspired by the shamanic shore birds of the Northwest coast with their distinctive beak shapes: the curved and compressed beak of the puffins and the wedge-shaped bill of the oyster catchers.

The sun also appears at the helm of *Into the Uncharted Bottomless Go the Brave Company Secure in their Flame's Vision* of 1994. At the prow is a shore bird with a wedge-shaped beak. Fish, integrated into the base of the boat, act as escorts for the trip. The passengers appear to be pale-faced Japanese ladies wearing blue kimonos and caps shaped as dark birds with rapier-like orange beaks, red eyes, and outstretched wings. Each of the ladies is wearing painted beads that serve as amulets and a necklace of simulated miniature brass containers. A small brass vase sits enigmatically at the base of the boat as if awaiting use in a ritual. A dozen or more small brass-coloured Chinese coins, medallion-like in appearance, are arranged in a row, ornamenting the gunwales of the boat on either side. Strakowski is interested in Asian culture and made a trip to Japan in 1986 where some of the embellishments were acquired as souvenirs. Here, as is the case with the series in general, the boat is a metaphor for a personal voyage during which the participants are always "taking a big chance." Frequently it is the boat that represents the artist. Its occupants are normally considered to be the artist's helpers during

the trip. Of course the boat is equipped with the requisite safety equipment of anchors and a flotation device.

In *Ritual for the Search of the Inner Passage* of 1989, the boat is a fish with four cats as passengers. Strakowski sees an affinity between fish and cats, perhaps because our relationship with them must be on their terms. At any rate, the two species are taking a trip together that the artist portrays as having a common goal. The cats are painted with clown-like faces of red, blue and white. They are wearing skeleton-like striped outfits that are painted and have necklaces of chicken bones. The skeletal or x-ray motif refers to bones being a symbol of regeneration to many cultures of the world. Indeed, one is tempted to consider the implications if the boat is deemed to be a personification of the artist.

In 2007 Strakowski completed *Odyssey* for her friend Georgette Paré. In this sculpture the figure at the helm of the craft represents Georgette; the occupants of the boat are family members. The work is exquisite in its detailing. The helmsperson is horned and her hair has a multitude of colourful beads woven into its braids. The outfits of the occupants are brightly painted with patterning that represents the birth animal of the wearer according to the Chinese calendar. Among the five occupants are her three children: Geneviève, Sarah, and Mathieu. Sarah and Mathieu are shown attached to their spouses, Keith and Karin respectively, with the charms they are wearing. Geneviève, at the front of the boat, is represented as a tiger. Sarah, in the middle, has an outfit patterned like a snake, while her husband Keith's is patterned like a tiger. Karin and Mathieu are both dragons.

  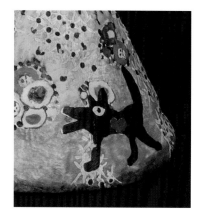 

After discussion with the family, the artist included Georgette's divorced husband Pierre in the tableau. He is represented as the horse clinging to the gunwale outside the boat near the bow. Just inside the boat beside him is a flotation ring. Strakowski provided the following verse as an extended title for the work:

> Odyssey
> flowing with one's innate sense of direction
> life's stage moves on
> While the actors wait for their cue.

As is the case with Strakowski's work in general, the adornment of the boat pieces greatly enhances their engagement with the viewer. Strakowski feels that her works provide a sense of history through the embellishments. On one level this is a personal history, to be sure, as viewers encounter the found objects in the sculptures as traces of the artist's own engagement with material culture. But Strakowski's collection of these objects and their use in her work may be in itself regarded as a ritualistic activity that is in harmony with and builds on the mythological themes of her subjects. Rituals are central to the mythologies that inform them, and the found objects may be regarded as the charms that are used in the service of her ritualistic practice. As Strakowski has stated, "we need the rituals because they affirm our place in the world." Thus on another more general level her work may speak to the need for mythology in our world, a mythology that stimulates a sense of mystery and wonderment.

Indeed, it may not be too much of a stretch to view the artist's own activity of collecting and using found objects in shamanic terms as a process of exchange between the mundane or day-to-day world and the realm of the spiritual or sacred.

Strakowski has noted the decline of cohesive ritualistic activities of the kind that strive to supersede the ordinary world in our contemporary society. For instance, the rite of passage for coming of age may be tied to getting a driver's license or entering licensed premises instead of ritualistic practices such as the Christian confirmation or Jewish bar mitzvah, which serve to connect and bind the initiate with a society through mythological rites. It is the close connection between ritual and society that entices Strakowski to make repeat visits to Mexico, where her mythic imagination has been stimulated by religious and other rituals, especially one of her favourite events, the Festival of the Dead. This celebration has inspired her both to make and to collect numerous works on the subject of death. Her washroom, for instance, has been embellished in the manner of a shrine. Among the colourful clutter of objects atop the toilet tank is a skeletal figure standing with hands clenched behind its neck wearing numerous necklaces. A small Amerindian wooden stool beside it reveals three small skulls. Standing on the floor beside the toilet is another skeleton wearing a black top hat. The three skulls on the wall shelf behind the tank are brightly painted in flower patterns. Squatting on one of them is a small skeleton holding a bright red fruit in its lap and wearing a crown and golden crucifix earrings. Another small skeleton lies atop the second skull. Out of the third

grows a tree with bright red fruit, symbolic of regeneration. Artificial flowers festoon the window adjacent to the toilet. A skeleton with a black cloak and staff is suspended like a marionette in the corner of the bathroom beside the window, and on a stool below it facing the toilet is yet another grinning skeleton wearing a pearl necklace, sunglasses, and a beret with an artificial flower. Atop the book case opposite the sink are more skeletons and skulls, and on the shelves in front of the books are numerous figurines – of celebrants, clowns, and musicians with their instruments fashioned from objects collected by the artist as souvenirs of her Mexican trips. The installation in her washroom is a vivid and effusive memento mori, festive and rather joyous, life-affirming rather than death-denying or dreading.

Pat Strakowski feels that our society needs to acknowledge death more than it does. In 1994, Strakowski and fellow Mexican traveller and artist Kirsten Abrahamson created the exhibition *Revival* at the Muttart Art Gallery in Calgary. The installation on the theme of death consisted of shrines, artificial flowers and numerous skeletons. At the time she described the Festival of the Dead as contrasting with our Canadian efforts at dealing with the subject of death: "They make it into a festival with fireworks, special food, special decorations, music, all night vigils in the cemetery … In our society, if someone is very ill or dies, we take them to the hospital or funeral home, and that's it." Her intent was to deal with death "as a continuous process, that from death comes life, and one is just as important as the other."[11] The ritual of embellishment is life-affirming: "In Mexico, the shrines and the churches are embellished

to excess, and I think that's right. Again, I believe to acknowledge death we must celebrate life."[12]

Strakowski's interest in myths that cross cultural boundaries recalls the ideas voiced by Joseph Campbell, an authority on mythology who was widely read in the 1980s; certainly Strakowski was thoroughly familiar with his ideas during the period she was emerging as an artist. For Campbell, myths are defined as "clues to the spiritual potentialities of the human life."[13] Underscoring this definition is the belief that one gains experience of life through the absorption of myths:

Read myths. They teach you that you can turn inward, and you begin to get the message of the symbols. Read other people's myths, not those of your own religion, because you tend to interpret your own religion in terms of facts – but if you read the other ones, you begin to get the message. Myth helps you to put your mind in touch with the experience of being alive. It tells you what the experience is.[14]

Campbell's comments resonate with Strakowski's interest in conveying life experiences. Strakowski considers herself to be a storyteller: "My inspirations come from life and the diversity of its form. Myths, legends, beliefs, traditions embellish them." Her medium is visual rather than verbal. She understands her life as a journey that underpins a personal storyline. Her collections of objects

 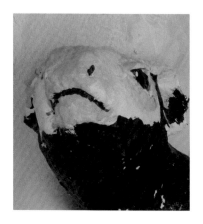  

serve as a reminder of life's experiences as well as being a catalyst for story development. She considers the mythology that she develops through her sculptures to be open in such a way that viewers can interpret them according to their own life experiences, and in the process acquire a mythological outlook. At the most she offers a title – a verbal clue – as an aid for relating to the work. The title itself is developed by the artist during the creation of her artwork and serves as a summary of her thought processes.

Strakowski, then, does not feel that her own concerns are imperative in understanding her work, which is richly veiled by complex and personal connotations. In this respect her views are consistent with the critical approaches of our contemporary era that focus on the visual image as capable of sustaining and conveying meaning beyond the intent of the artist. If one views visual art as a language, the artist's intent becomes but one of a number of components and complex interactions that include the viewer's background, the message conveyed, the formal code, the medium of expression, and the historical and socio-political context of the work. The understanding of visual images as a language owes much to semiotics, the study of signs and symbols, an influence that was making rapid strides in the art world when Strakowski was attending the College.

Two important critics who have profoundly influenced the art world, Roland Barthes, a 20th century French literary and social theorist; and Jacques Derrida (1930-2004), the founder of desconstruction theory, have created analytical frameworks which enable Strakowski's work to be interpreted in the wider context of modern art.

To Roland Barthes, the analysis begins with the study of language, which he sees as operating at two levels: literal and symbolic. Literal meaning is continually and immediately affected by symbolic content that he referred to as "myth." Myth thus becomes a "type of speech, a system of communication."[15] Furthermore, the relationship between the mythical and literal level of language "can only be explained by reference to a larger social field, a social field that is structured in terms of class interests and values."[16] Symbolic activity that leads to mythical meaning is culturally relevant. Thus viewing Strakowski's work as a language forces a grounding of myth itself in an individual's cultural background in the symbolic interpretation of the work. In other words, as Strakowski herself intends, the meaning in her work is open to interpretation.

Take as an example the sculpture *About Angels, Flights of Imagination, and Other Grey Areas* of 2006. The title is enigmatic, but the imagery of the work itself readily acknowledges a reading of literal meaning and an interpretation of symbolic meaning. At the literal level the reading is of a figure clothed in ostrich feathers, standing on a spiralling carpet and using its hands to lift its head above its body. However, these literal meanings surrender immediately to symbolic association. This second level of meaning varies according to the viewer's cultural background and personal history. In my case, I see a figure enmeshed in a vortex about to stick its head in the sand to avoid the consequences of some unknown act;

the spiralling carpet has become a symbol of the vortex while the ostrich feathers signify avoidance. To me the work alludes to both the elation and doubt associated with the creative process in which the artist is either shirking the call of the muse or attempting to take a breather from this call.

Certainly, Strakowski's work is a product of its time. Even though her work might be interpreted as slightly odd or idiosyncratic, it cannot be perceived as out of touch with contemporary issues. Moreover, her upbringing in an ethnically diverse milieu and her mythological interests that cross cultural boundaries make a discussion in this context relevant. The act of communication in a culturally pluralistic society is enriched or impoverished, depending on one's point of view – and clearly Strakowski prefers the former notion – because it becomes less likely there will be one dominant reading of information at the mythical level.

Integral to the analysis is a consideration of how we receive myths by categorizing three types of interpreters: the "journalist", the "mythologist", and the "reader". The journalist "starts with a concept and seeks a form for it" and the mythologist "deciphers the myth, he understands a distortion."[17] These two processes "are static, analytical." The reader, on the other hand, consumes myth in a dynamic manner, living the myth "as a story at once true and unreal."[18] The development of Strakowski's work is certainly dynamic in this sense of the myth reader. The act of artistic creation is an open process ungoverned by undue

preconception or analysis. Concept and form evolve together as one action leading to another. The title of the work evolves in the process of the making. Similarly, one work leads to another in a story reflecting life experiences and interactions. The continuous, unrelenting, and effusive nature of the adornment in Strakowski's works – the embellishment of her story – manifests the needs of a myth reader. It is "speech justified in excess."[19]

This is a dynamic process – the continual interchange between form and concept through which literal meaning succumbs to symbolic meaning.[20] In Strakowski's work this interplay is not only dynamic but also contributes to considerable dialectical tension – that is, the clash of opposites. This tension is apparent in the polarization that occurs when objects from the mundane world, from popular culture, are incorporated into visual art, in the process creating an opposition between the "low" and the "high".

Another seeming opposition in her work is between the sacred and profane. This tension, however, is more apparent than actual, and can be resolved by applying the deconstruction concept that Jacques Derrida used to challenge conventional Western metaphysical notions of what is real. Conventionally, our conceptual order is based on a classification system of yes/no, either/or oppositions that govern our thinking. Refuting this is the idea of "undecidables" – the premise that concepts can exist that include within themselves aspects normally seen as mutually incompatible. Pop art is an example of this principle, incorporating found objects and/or images into art. The found objects of Pop art may be read either as popular culture or

art. They are undecidable. Traditional oppositions such as high/low, and sacred/profane become irresolvable in the process:

> It's a move that avoids the traditional polarized readings, e.g. EITHER Pop Art as an investigative analysis of popular culture, a "truth drug"; OR Pop Art is as vacuous, uniform and ephemeral as the kitsch it imports – an "opiate of the masses." If we treat its objects as undecidable, we're disturbing the oppositional distinctions on which these polarized readings are founded.[21]

Spirit Guides in their Magic Craft, examined here earlier, is a good example with which to discuss this disturbance to oppositional thinking. The gummed stickers on the outfit of the ancient lady seem to disrupt the magical aura of the work. Objects from the mundane world seem to intrude into what is otherwise a spiritual realm. This aspect of the work brings up the sacred/profane dichotomy. Similarly, the vestigial figure that is neither here nor there, neither becoming nor vanishing, advances the presence/absence opposition. However, if the vestigial figure and gummed stars are treated as *undecidables*, the foundations of our conceptual order are now questioned. The vestigial figure as an undecidable challenges the automatic favouring of presence over absence; the gummed stars as an undecidable disrupt the opposition of the sacred to the profane. The latter result depicts a modern condition in which this opposition is losing currency

and mimics a common critical outlook of our contemporary era. Strakowski presents a worldview in which the objects of our world are perpetually enmeshed in mythological communication that is at once "true and unreal," to borrow Barthes's phrase discussed earlier. The roles of the spiritual and mundane in her work are not oppositional but relational, inextricably linked in an ongoing exchange – not unlike the shamanic relationship between the sacred and profane, but without attachment to a specific culture, in keeping with Strakowski's global perspective. By remaining open to meaning in this relational rather than oppositional manner, Strakowski's works are gently subversive.

In Strakowski's studio there are a number of works of folk art. Two that stand out are mixed media sculptures: one, *San Simón,* by an anonymous Guatemalan artist; and the other, *Mr. T,* by Canadian artist George Markel. San Simón is a sinister-looking character. Seated in a wooden chair, he wears an old, crumpled, wide-brimmed hat and has a cigarette stuffed between lips half-hidden behind a thick moustache. The ashen colour of his wooden body contrasts strongly with his festive attire. He wears a dark-blue suit and has numerous objects draped around his neck: brightly coloured sashes adorned with geometric patterns and several necklaces with beads ranging from small to large. Resting against his knee is a wooden staff. San Simón (also known as Maximón), a contemporary cult figure popular in rural Guatemala, is a hybrid character representing aspects of both ancient Mayan beliefs and Roman Catholicism. The Maya believed in nature deities; when they adopted Christianity, characteristics of those deities

   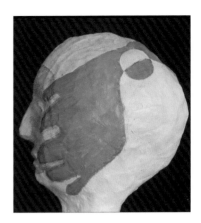

were superimposed onto Christian figures. The striking difference in the two belief systems is apparent in the San Simón figure. The Maya included gods representing the darker forces of nature in their worship. Normally, the Christian representation would be of Roman Catholic saints, presumably the embodiment of holiness, but here there is a further opposition – the Guatemalans sometimes associate Judas Iscariot, a personna who to Christians is symbolic of evil, to live on in San Simón. Indeed, San Simón may be understood as an undecidable, disrupting the Christian/heathen and good/evil oppositions.

Markel's standing sculpture *Mr. T* portrays a character from popular culture. Mr. T emerged as a professional wrestler and actor in the 1980s in tough-guy characters such as "Clubber" Lang the boxer in the movie Rocky III. Markel shows Mr. T with his signature traits: a Mohawk hairstyle and large amounts of gold jewellery. Barthes's concept of myth as "speech justified in excess" certainly applies here in both form and subject. The fact that these examples of folk art are prominently displayed in her own collection indicates that such work has been influential in her development.

Pat Strakowski has often been referred to as a folk artist. Certainly, her work does have stylistic similarities to both *Mr. T* and *San Simón*. It has the "look" of folk art. *Momdonna II* of 2006, for instance, presents a standing mother clutching her child. She is from a series of Madonnas that Strakowski terms "other wise women." As in the works of folk art, the mother and child are embellished with objects and materials readily found in the day-to-day world. The figures are dressed in upholstery remnants that create a pleasingly textured and

coloured effect. The top of the mother's dress is fringed with a variety of doll-like miniature figurines. She wears dangling gold earrings and a large red and green beaded necklace. Her cap of gold, red, and green materials has a crow-like bird perched on top. The facial features of the mother and child are simply differentiated as in the folk art figures *San Simon* and *Mr. T*. The title of the work is a play on the Italian root of *donna*, literally meaning "lady". The term "Madonna", normally referring to the Virgin Mary, has been here seemingly demystified to underscore the mother and child as a more common phenomenon.

Strakowski, like many folk artists, often turns to popular culture for inspiration. A striking example of this is a pair of works that advances the commonplace and acts as a personification of Calgary or "Cowtown": the Cowboy and Cowgirl in the "Prairie Minder" series – called *Tall Prairie Grass Racer* and *Season of Renewal* respectively – of 1998. These two standing figures are juxtaposed in her studio with some bird decoys. Both figures wear the typical attire of the cowboy. His wide-brimmed hat is embellished with a star, hers with an exotic-looking golden butterfly-like ornament. They both wear buckskin vests, jeans, and boots. He totes a six-shooter and his string tie is held in place by a white cow-skull. What makes the works so appealing and funny are the calf she clutches against her abdomen and the galloping horse that he holds in his right hand. The incongruous relationship in scale between the figures and animals enhances the imaginative appeal of the works.

Folk art has been often associated with the vernacular expressions of untutored artists. However, the opposition of the words

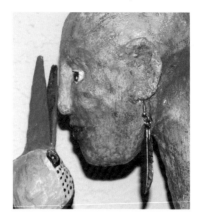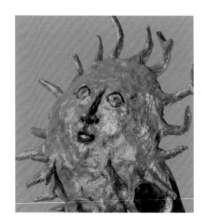

"folk" and "art" in the classification creates a dichotomy between the commonplace and the exalted, or the low and the high.[22] Strakowski is a well-trained and well-read artist. Her ready association with folk art points to a resistance in accepting the dictates of fine art.

Two well-known contemporary critics, Michael Hall and Donald Kuspit, have offered comments on this phenomenon. Hall, an American sculptor, has argued that both folk artists and so-called "fine artists" work in the same cultural continuum and that their art has common ends: "Art at both the high end and low end is cognition and context…. Projected and focused, the images artists make express the concerns which intellectually, temperamentally and spiritually identify an age…"[23] However, what is most revealing in regards to Strakowski is Donald Kuspit's evaluation of Hall's ideas: "While… Hall argues persuasively for folk art and high art as two sides of the same cultural coin, it is folk art rather than high art that seems to suggest a greater sense of realization of self, for it seems more creative in itself, and suggests the creativity of the society at large rather than of a specialized group of creators called artists."[24] This insight provides an explanation not only for Strakowski's interest in folk art but also for popular culture as a catalyst for her work. She is more interested in the larger cultural sphere as fodder for her myth-making than in the potentially more restrictive confines of fine art.

Among the mythic characters in her studio stands the *Eclectic Visionary* of 1998. She wears a robe of royal blue, open and tied at the waist with a red sash. The colour gold predominates. Golden stars and planetary bodies, and a light-blue cherub adorn the robe. A golden orb hangs on a chain, a large set of keys dangles from the waist. She casts her glance heavenward with parted lips as if in wonderment. Her face is a golden disc and she has the familiar representations of the sun's face and its rays attached in relief for eyes. Finial projections from her head create a star-like hairdo. A dove glides down over one of the finials towards the top of her head.

The eclectic visionary reaches out for the world-at-large, even further to the cosmos, as far as the reach will allow. As long as there is form to entertain meaning, she will strive to advance a mythology of being. Never stationary, she is always on the move in an effort to exchange our worldly trappings for further insight, until the earthly flame flickers and extinguishes.

It is now May Day. Early signs of spring are everywhere in Calgary. I look forward to a visit with Pat to share this manuscript. Now in her early seventies, she considers the yard as her spring and summer passion. A multitude of brightly coloured bird houses dot the trees and garage. Soon the Virginia creeper and clematis will come alive on the trellis covering the outside patio. A variety of ferns will sprout in the shaded areas of the yard. An admirer of the variety of textures and subtle shades of hostas, she has a large plot of these to eagerly anticipate. There are also plots for flowers, both cultivated and wild, and wild grasses. Her outdoor world will become a location of wonderment much like her studio.

The Art of Pat Strakowski

This sculpture started with the ostrich feathers, which I found in a dumpster. I thought, obviously these don't want to be in the garbage, so I rescued them, I kept them for years and years and finally this sculpture came along. This is one of my pieces where I leave everything open for the viewer. I like people to make their own interpretation. For instance, if you look at the head straight on it has a look of anguish, but if you look at it from the side view it's OK – it's not anguished at all. And why is the figure taking his head off? Well, why wouldn't he? It's about imagination pondering freedom from heavy loads. You want to be free but your hands are holding you down.

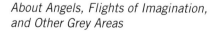

About Angels, Flights of Imagination,
and Other Grey Areas

This is a creature that provides things you need for life. It provides clothing, it provides food. That's why he has a spoon, you won't go hungry. It can also be a guardian figure or protector. I've worked in some found objects like antlers, some driftwood for the spoon. The mane is made out of linen thread. I used off-loom weaving techniques to connect the fibres to the figure. I like the feel of linen thread, it has a nice surface, it doesn't look machine-made, it knots nicely.

The Provider

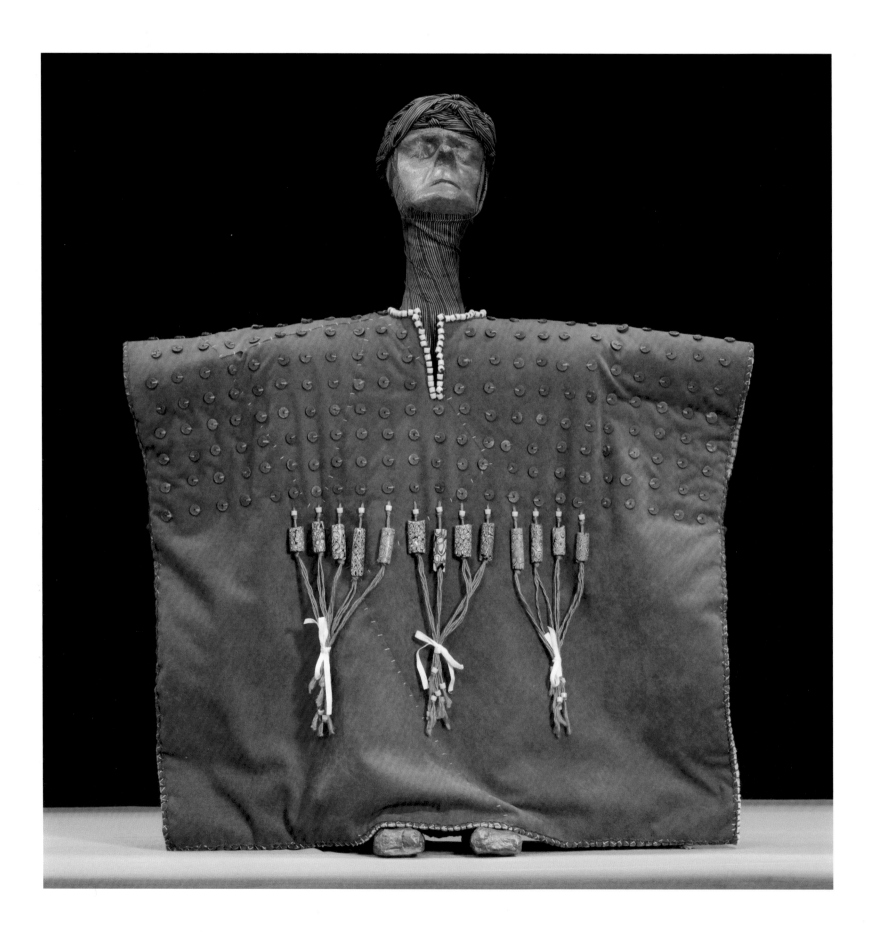

This is a piece from my first large series, from the early 1980s. I was very interested in costuming and working with textures and reflective surfaces. I'd also started using found objects – trade beads and fragments of fabric and different kinds of embellishments, things I call "neat stuff." I had an awful lot of things that I could use. I liked the idea of rich colour and rich surface, to suggest affluence, possibly someone who was royal. Then, adding something dull to something that is bright, to something that is soft, you have a flow of one kind of texture to another. But it all depends on how you look at it – when you are working with different types of surfaces you get a different kind of image depending on the lighting and the time of day.

Ancestor 12

This is an odyssey, the ladies are flying to their destination. It's a flying boat, almost like a space ship. The ladies look Japanese, I didn't intend that, that's just the way it turned out. When I visited Japan I was influenced by Noh theatre and kabuki. Maybe that's why their faces are so white and they have funny hats. The "flame's vision", that's the sun, and the ladies are pursuing its vision. They are following a path and the sun gives them the light so they can find their way. They don't know their destination, they won't know until they get there. The birds on their heads fly off to look for land and when they find land they stay. If they don't find it they'll come back, but they are confident they will find whatever is their destination.

Into the Uncharted Bottomless Go the Brave Company, Secure in their Flame's Vision

Following page: Details

In 1988 I was part of a Christmas show at the Virginia Christopher Gallery in Calgary. For this exhibition I created at least a dozen figures. Some were people, some anthropomorphic figures, some monsters, devils and such. They were about 25-35 cms tall. They were all celebrating the holiday season.

Ginger

*I made **Deformed Angel I** after the twin towers in New York were bombed on 9/11. The figure represents the twin towers and they are going up in smoke and it's the whole world looking on and on the mask you see the hand across the mouth and the tear because to me it was such a tragedy and I felt that it was all based on money and this is why you see coins on the bottom. So this is why to me it is a representation of 9/11.*

Deformed Angel 1

I created this piece for my studio. I made the white mask, which is like a sentry piece, and I made the horns, and for the body I glued pieces of a wasps' nest. I incorporate wasps' nests into my figures whenever I get them, usually from my friends. I like the texture and I like the colour. Wasps' nests aren't a solid colour, they could have blacks and greys and sometimes they have a blue tint depending on where they got the material to make the nest. But anyway, that's the natural colour of the nest on the body of the figure. When I get the wasps' nest I store it in a plastic bag, then I peel layers off it very gently, otherwise within a week or so it would start falling apart. I created this figure starting with dowel and chicken wire and then I covered it with the papier-mâché . And then when that dried I used the wasps' nest. It's like peeling an onion. You have to be very careful because the material is very thin. It's almost like tissue paper, it's so fragile. I'll wet the figure first and then I'll apply the wasps' nest very gently on the figure and then I'll kind of pat it to the form. It's almost like using gold leaf. I use an acrylic medium working in small areas about two inches by two inches. You wet that area with the medium and then you gently apply the wasps' nest. I use a sponge or you can use your fingers but you have to be very careful. Once the medium dries it won't crumble away.

Deformed Angel 3

The key thing with **Eclectic Visionary**, she's got a mask, and there are no eyes because I feel that the visionary instead of looking out, is looking inward. She has this robe that has stars, keys and different kinds of beadwork, moons and suns. These are the things that will protect her. There is a bird and the bird represents vision. It can also be the soul. But basically when I created this piece I wanted to say that a visionary doesn't necessarily have to look outward. A lot of times a visionary looks inward because they have to go into their own strengths and resources to come up with the solutions to whatever is happening and the keys that unlock certain doors. So she has several keys. She also has coins because in a lot of mythology you need coins, maybe for paying the ferry man or when you meet certain people who give you tasks. You usually have to exchange something and a lot of times it's coins.

Eclectic Visionary

Following pages: Detail

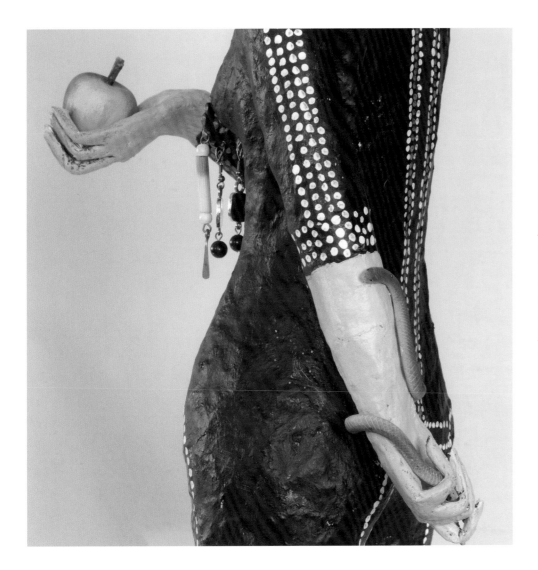

Lilith appears in the Books of the Apocrypha. Adam and Lilith were made out of mud and God gave them life. Lilith wanted to be on top and Adam complained to God that that wasn't fair so God banished Lilith by banishing her from Eden. God then made Adam fall asleep and he made Eve from his ribs. So Eve was always second, she was not equal to Adam, which translated that women were not equal to men. I have Lilith holding an apple – and to me the apple represents knowledge. She's got a hand behind her back and she's holding a stick – well, you know, when you start telling stories they change every time. Different people tell the same story so what happens is the stick becomes a snake. And so I have her holding a green stick behind her back. It's like the snake is a symbol of regeneration in a story that changes all the time. It was a stick originally but you know now it becomes a snake because snakes are something we don't like – there's all kinds of negative stuff with snakes.

Facing page:
Lilith: Third Transformation;
Deformed Angel II;
Wisdom Comes from Seeing the World
  from a Different Point of View

This page:
Detail from *Lilith: Third Transformation*

*I started out with **Deformed Angel I** after the 9/11 attack [see page 36]. **Deformed Angel II** is about the people sent to war as the result of 9/11. In front of the figure there is a tree with a lot of yellow ribbons tied to it. The figure is wearing a dog tag which is a symbol identifying the soldiers that were sent to war. A lot of them didn't come back and a lot of them that came back were damaged – this is why I call them deformed angels, why I call this one **Deformed Angel II**. John [Heintz], when he was taking the photographs, had a terrible time focusing the face, and he couldn't figure out what the problem was. I told him that the face is not meant to be in focus. I smudged a lot because I wanted to give it that look that it isn't new, it is worn, it is old, it is damaged. One side of its face gives it a sort of Renaissance look where you have something that is very old and the wind and the elements weather it so that it's not really in focus.*

Detail from *Deformed Angel II*

*I call this one **Wisdom Comes from Seeing the World from a Different Point of View**. This came about when some of us were talking about wisdom and how you went about getting it. Some people say you have to experience a lot of things, or you have to have the maturity or age, and I thought well, a better explanation is to see things from a different point of view – that is how you gain wisdom.*

Detail from *Wisdom Comes from Seeing the World from a Different Point of View*

The Beaver Women fit in a North American mythology, not West Coast or Prairie, but a mythology of my own, sort of a general symbol of Canadian history. I like working in multiples, especially if I'm working with small figures because they tend to disappear if they're all by themselves. When I'm doing a series I start with the same shape, I'll paint and embellish each one differently, and when I have a number of them, they make quite a strong image. Originally I made about 20 of the Beaver Women. I don't keep that accurate a number. When I'm working on a series based on one figure, it's a case of one looking like this, one looking like that. When I run out of steam I stop. These three are the only ones left, I don't know where the others are.

Beaver Women

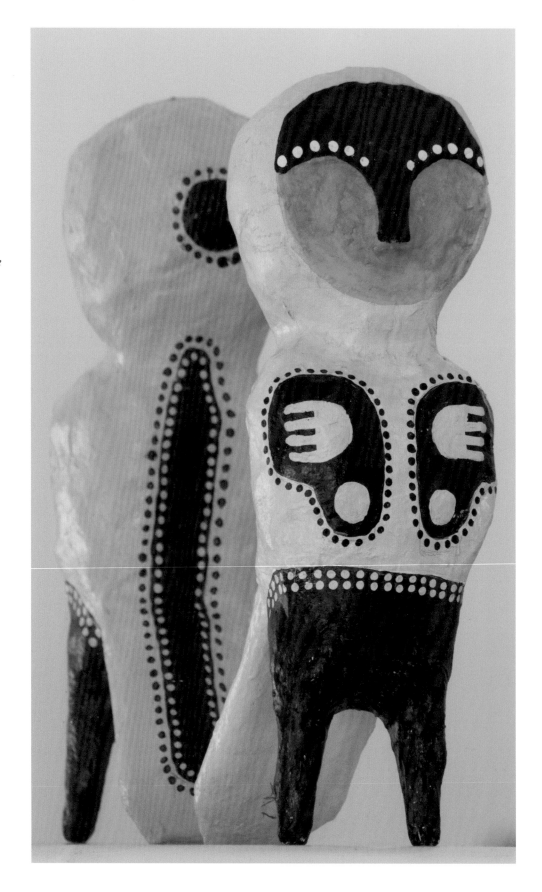

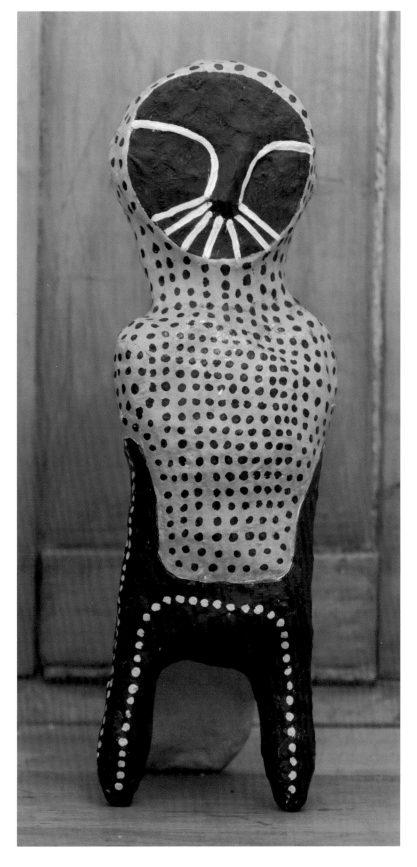

Converging to the Point of Most Familiar Origin

These are wise women, flying to their destination, using a bird to take them to their destination. They're on a quest – or maybe they're going home, probably going to their centre, I'm not sure. These are people you don't mess with, they're not kindly or sweet, like all my sculptures they have their own personae.

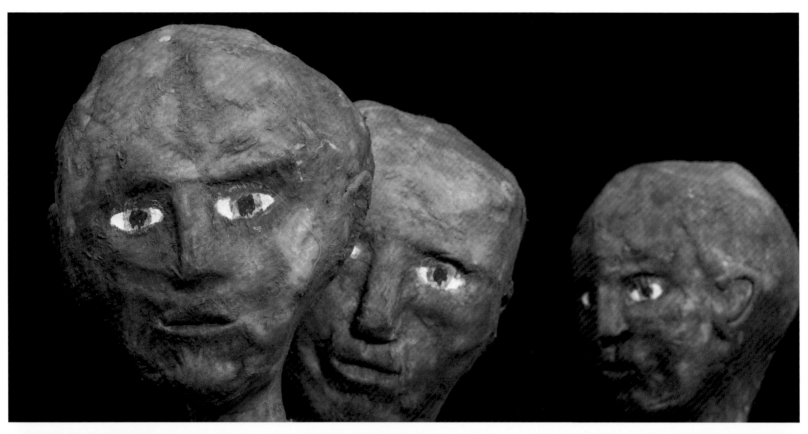

This is another of my deer figures. Part of the mythology of the prairies is they have all these wonderful deer, but you don't see them because they're very short, they're only about this big, so if you're driving by you're not going to see them, they're very shy. This one has a mane like a lion, he looks like a devil. Maybe he has special powers?

Dwarf Prairie Shorthorn

This is another deer that lives on the prairie. This one is quite a bit fancier. He has 10 prongs. He has hair coming down. I used linen fibre and wove that right on the figure. He is quite proud. He is also quite shy, so you don't see him often. Deer like the bushes and the trees. If they sit still you won't notice them. Some people say the horns look like snakes and ask if this was a medusa figure, or if the prong on the head is a devil symbol. Sometimes they even ask if I worship demons; I tell them, "I think you have a problem."

Dwarf Prairie 10 Prong

*I call this one **In Collaboration** because I worked on it with another artist, Ilse Anysas-Salkauskas.*Ilse and I were in several shows and we thought that to give the show more impact – you know, both of us are pushing boundaries – we collaborated on a sculpture. So I made two sculptures and then Ilse decorated both sculptures so the leather work is Ilse's and the sculptures are mine. Now the way we went about this is I started with the sculpture and then I painted it and gave it to Ilse and then Ilse used her leather work . Then she would give the sculpture back to me and I would add to it and then I would give it back to her. If she wanted to add to it she would give it back to me and I would do the finishing touches. It's a matter of passing the works back and forth and when we get to the last stage we give it our final touch. Ilse's looks similar to mine but her colours are different and her embellishments are different. Ilse's face isn't painted like mine, the turtle and the deer figure painted on the face. She gave me extra leather for the hat. I made the hat and I added bells and the beads. We each have one sculpture. I was probably the principal force, so to speak, on my sculpture. Ilse was the principal force on hers. It's a very good experience because I find when you collaborate, you get ideas that you had never thought of, and you give each other ideas.*

* Ilse Anysas-Salkauskas and Pat Strakowski, along with a third artist, Liv Pedersen, formed the travelling group "The Three Muses".

In Collaboration

Following page: Detail

This is about death. It's like the last dance with the woman in black. She cuts your mortal coil, hence the skulls around the neck, yes. The bluebird in her hands is the soul. At the base you have snakes and ladders, you know, from the games where you have a ladder you go up and you have a snake you go down. It's about life's adventure. The woman is dressed in a tuxedo but in the back she has a bustle that looks like a lace skirt. So even though she is a lady in black it could be male or it could be female but the idea is that it's your last dance and this is your partner.

Lady in Black

In our culture death is quite a taboo subject, but it's not like that everywhere. In Mexico, for instance, they celebrate death. They have the Festival of the Dead. It's a big celebration, they have special foods, dances and fireworks, all kinds of exhibitions. Everywhere you go you would see displays and decorations. You go to a book store and you'd see a skeleton reading a book, and you'd go to a park and you'd see a young couple dressed like skeletons. You would have a mother and father and a baby in a stroller and a dog and they would all be skeletons. It was such a joyful celebration, people could look at their own mortality and not feel that this is it, the end is terrible. It is not terrible. Mexicans believe death is not the end, it's part of the great life cycle, out of death would come birth, would come life. My sculpture tries to show that. It is a memory shell because this is where you keep your memory. Trees grow out of the skull, the plant is a rebirth, a new life. It is renewal. You have your chance. You wait your turn, but you have to make room for the next generation.

Memory Shell - Renewal of the Great Cycle

Harvest Moon is about the harvest and how we celebrate abundance so you will see fields that have been ploughed and are waiting for the spring again. The face is actually a moon face shining on the landscape and here on the base you will see animal tracks and the landscape as it appears from a distance. The beads could be foodstuffs. When you have a plentiful harvest it's not just like one thing it's the idea of plenty of everything – it's different foods and ornamental gourds and all that. But it's the idea that you are celebrating a successful harvest, so the beads signify wealth.

Harvest Moon

This is a shaman piece. The idea of guardians and shamans comes from the North American Indians. Any time something happened to a person they would seek a shaman. The shaman could predict the future of the tribe. The reason it has two heads, it's the idea of the alter ego. In addition, like anyone else, the shaman also needs a guardian, so it's got these two. Now they could be male/female. They could be both male, or both female, or they could be the real or the spiritual. It's up to you to interpret this. When I created this I used leather for the pieces and these little bells I had to construct from lids from cans of salmon. I had to find the right canned salmon because these lids had to be brass ones. Some of the salmon lids didn't have the brass. I needed that reflective surface and the noise and sounds because these are the things that give the shaman power where you have the power of light and the power of the noise that the bells make.

Spirit Guide

*The reason I have a girl skipping and call it **Spring Ritual** is that I think this is one way we learn life's lessons. When I was a child we would skip rope but we would also say verses like "tinker tailor soldier sailor rich man poor man beggar man thief." You kept skipping and skipping and repeating this and then whoever you ended up with was who you would marry, which wasn't true but it's part of the ritual. When I was thinking of **Spring Ritual** I was focusing on the idea of spring and things growing up. Plants and growing things make me feel rejuvenated. The girl is exuberant – these forms coming out of her head are what she is imagining while she is skipping. When I made the skipping rope I had to find a cable that was strong enough to hold the sculpture up. Then I wrapped the cable with fabric and painted it. The base was also painted to look like a sidewalk and I have little ants and things like that because you know in the springtime you see all sorts of bugs and things.*

Spring Ritual

*I was working on a series of saints and I was reading a book about people who became saints. It seems no one really started life wanting to become one. It's usually the person for some reason or other thought that there was a wrong and they would go against authority and in turn they would be punished. Then people would treat them as a martyr. I'm not talking about any particular person. Saints appear in many shapes, sizes, and forms. Now this one, **Saint Luna of the Night Light**, is actually the moon. The dark studded jacket is representative of stars and the black and white squares on the leg are a decoration that can be interpreted as a road or how you see farmers' fields at night when you see a light area and a dark area. Usually farms are in squares or rectangles so this is what I thought of. These little studs coming around her as a crown, these too are stars.*

Saint Luna of the Night Light

I chose the name because with the long skinny legs it looks like it's doing the "spider walk". When I did it [1985] I was taken by Japanese culture, for instance Kabuki theatre. They have these costumes with all these bulky sleeves and ornamentation so you don't know how big the figure is. I wanted to accentuate the tall and skinny, which is why I included the hat. Instead of making the hat absolutely straight I thought I would twist it a bit to make it kind of whimsical and funny. Then I added the cloth from Afghanistan and embellished it with the raffia pom-poms. In the end it doesn't really look like a Kabuki piece at all, but something out of my imagination.

Spider Walk

The Whyte Museum in Banff used to have the "Myth of Exceptional Pass" shows every few years and this was in the 1985 show. Actually this was my first boat and the story behind it is that the spirits would come on their magic craft but instead of landing on the water they would land in the trees and this is why they are in this nest-like craft where you could put them on top of a tree. What I used here was old bean vines from my parents' garden. I made them like a wreath with a small hole in the middle so they can park on top of the trees. This was the idea of these mystical figures and their mystical craft because of the theme around the myth of Exceptional Pass where wonderful things happen. Regarding the two figures, the one painted dark blue with the stars is for the night and the light-coloured one is for the day. I used natural elements, porcupine quills and bits of drift wood, to embellish the figures and give them a kind of mythical quality.

Spirit Guides in their Magic Craft

Sedna's Fashion Statement

This is a "Sedna" figure I created after I went to Iqaluit in 2008 to do a papier-mâché workshop for the stone carvers and other artists living there. This was a wonderful experience because it wasn't like a workshop. It was a situation where I would show artists what they could do with paper. They were really amazed: "That is paper?" Yes, that is paper. "And that is paper?" Yes. They just couldn't believe it. Once they saw how easy and how cheap it was – well, I'm hoping in two or three years you are going to see papier-mâché coming out of the North. That would be really wonderful. Anyways, this is **Sedna's Fashion Statement**. Sedna is a very important figure in Inuit mythology. She is a goddess of the sea, the seals and the fish and the whales – they all came from Sedna. They have great respect for her; if you insult her she may hold back the bounty of the sea. She has a seal-like body but I gave her a human face, then I embellished her with all kinds of things. I used off-loom weaving to braid her beautiful long hair. Then I attached the embellishments. These shells with holes cut in them, I've had them for God knows how many years and at last I found a use for them. I also put in shells and driftwood and bottle tops and bits of bottle and maybe a bead or something, things you would see if you went beachcombing. So this is why I embellished her the way that I did – she's making a fashion statement.

This piece, ***Identity Protected by Memory Beads***, was in the Alberta Craft Council's "Going Green" travelling show that went around the province for three years. The theme of the show was recycling. The idea was that you recycle things or elements in things rather than get new things. So with this piece, I gave it a necklace of different found objects like beads or wood or things that are recycled. And I think it's a short step from the idea of recycling to the idea of memory, so the beads that she's wearing are memory beads and as you get older you have to have symbols that help you to remember. So this is why this figure is wearing the memory beads. Sometimes you forget your identity and this is a means of protecting yourself. Then the glass beads and wooden beads and metal beads continue as blue and white beads painted on her body. You can see that these beads are loose – they're kind of falling. She is standing on the base, and it's like you're opening up to another dimension and she is standing touching the sky and the stars. I continued this idea with the bird's face. If you look at the face from one way you'll see the bird's eye is also the figure's eye but then when you look around the back to the other side you see the wings. It's like the bird is flying across the face but in such a way that rather than hiding the face it's going around the back and then you can see it on both sides. On one side you see the wings and on the other you see the head.

Identity Protected by Memory Beads

Next page: Details

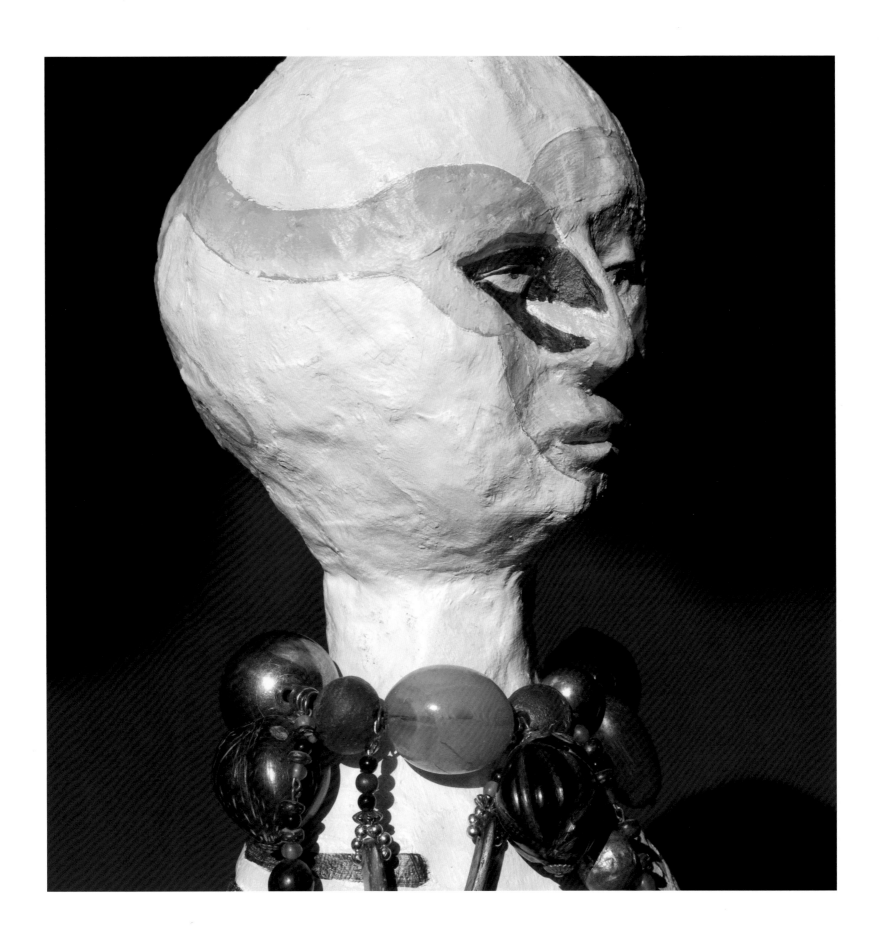

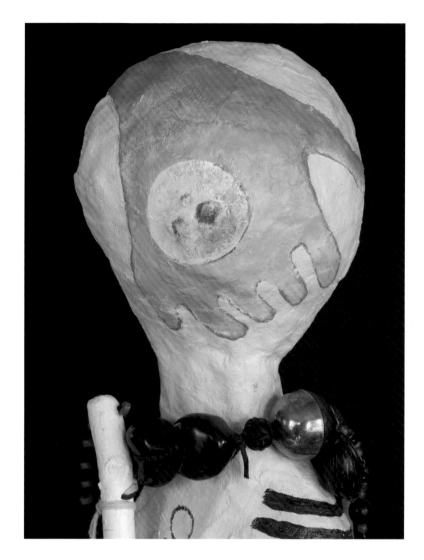
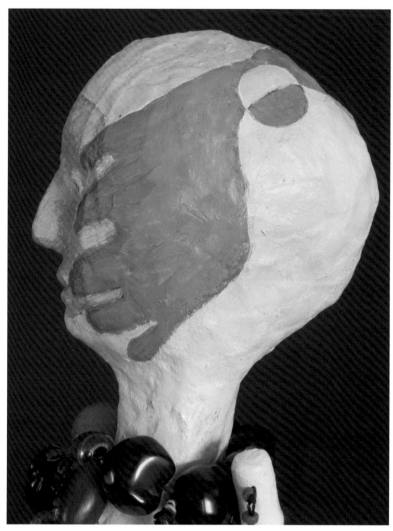

This is **Mandonna**. Now a few years before I did these madonna pieces I was in a show called "Saints and Sinners". I started to study madonnas and then I felt, well you don't just need a madonna, you need a **Mud**donna and a **Moon**donna, and a **Mom**donna. Now this is **Man**donna, he's got these sunglasses, because I thought, if you're a mandonna, this is the way you'd look. He's got this superman tie because naturally the mandonna is a superman, and he's got a donut on his head which is actually a halo and he's also standing in the clouds. The reflections in the window shows he's multi-dimensional, not just a figure in a kind of sterile setting like a studio with a white background. When you have a reflection you give another dimension to the figure, to the way it looks.

Mandonna

The Cohorts

When I started on the boat series, it was quite simple. You would have a boat and a figure and that was that. Then I started thinking about what the boats meant. The idea generally was you were crossing the unknown, you needed a helper, you would have people helping you but you would also need charms and things like that to make sure the voyage was safe. The cohorts are warrior types, they are guardians, they have shields and they are well armed. I portrayed them as deer figures, anthropomorphic figures with deer horns. The Norse and Germanic pagans believed that deer were sacred because they communicated with the gods through their horns. They could also be North American aboriginal – my images are not obviously one culture or the other, I mix the cultures and kind of adopt them as my own.

This is the idea of the moon moving in the sky and it's moving across the earth. I like to add a little bit of fantasy to my figures so the face is a moon face and it's got hands and the hands are moving with the figure like someone in water floating and their hands are trailing behind. The front embellishment is like a Venetian blind, you're looking out the window and you're seeing the moon pass. These white marks are — actually I don't know what they are, I just thought they would look good on this piece. The light dots on the hands look kind of nice and these easily could be stars or planets. The red dot on the base with the yellow vertical stripes, well, maybe these don't signify anything, but if you want they could very well signify the idea of a figure sleeping, it's got a blanket with stripes on it and there's the moon moving across the earth. The red dot on the face counterbalances the red ones in the hands. Originally I painted my bases black and I got to the point where I wanted to change that. A lot of my recent figures have painted bases so they blend better with each other.

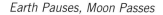

Earth Pauses, Moon Passes

Facing page:
Every Day is a Good Day When
   You're Above Ground;
Momdonna II;
Enchantment Leads to
   That Which Delights the Eye

This piece was originally made for the 1994 show at the Muttart Gallery called the "Revival Show". This was inspired by my going to Mexico for the first time in the early nineties to view the Day of the Dead celebrations. Now what happened was that this figure was created then but at some point I changed the embellishments and I added the little angel. I was thinking about the idea of getting old and dying and considering life and that every day is a good day when you're above ground. I like the idea of this angel coming from the inside – it's the idea of new life because in Mexico they believe that death is not final. They believe that out of death comes life – it's rebirth, so that when your turn is up you must pass away to make room for the new generation.

Every Day is a Good Day
When You're Above Ground

This is **Momdonna II**, she is the second **Momdonna**. When I created her I was working on a series where I had **Man**donna and **Mud**donna and **Moon**donna and **Mere**donna, all plays on the word "madonna". I was kind of curious about the different interpretations of "madonnas". So I thought, "madonna" originally meant a woman of high birth, and that gave me freedom to make this figure rich. I thought, let's explore this momdonna theme. This figure is holding a child, and she's got this ribbon that's coiled on top of her head that's like a crown but it's a bird's nest, and you see this bird, a blackbird that likes shiny things and hides them in the nest. The momdonna has spoons for earrings. These mean she and her children will never go hungry – this is an earth mother. Is there any connection with Mary and Christ? No. There could be, but I don't want it to go there, I didn't interpret it that way.

Momdonna II

When I was creating this figure, I was thinking in terms of beauty and it's also a cultural thing. Some cultures would like a lot of tattooing and other cultures would cover the face. It's the idea of what is your perception of beauty, and your perception of beauty depends on you and your culture. So I created this figure with all the embellishments, like around the neck, and this wide belt with these beautiful glass Viennese beads. That it's the idea that beauty is also part of enchantment. This is a thing that is like an attraction figure. If you are enchanting you are considered beautiful and desirable. She's got her hands raised, so at some point she will probably rise and do a dance. The hands are an important factor. People pay a lot of attention to the hands and the gesture of the fingers.

Enchantment Leads to That Which Delights the Eye

In 2007 the Alberta Society of Artists had a hat show and they invited the artists to participate by creating a hat. I was wondering what kind of a hat to make. I'm not a hat wearer but I know that hats are symbolic of, say, your station in life or if you belong to a group. Hats are even like crowns – they signify something or someone that is very important. So when I created this piece I just wanted to have a lot of fun. I made a top hat with hands and bands with embellishments – I have the moon and tin found objects and in the front I have this hand that I think is made out of beaten tin. There's an eye in the hand that I got in Mexico. They have a lot of these tin embellishments – they use them for photographs. So I made this hat for the Hat Project.

Grandmaster's Hat for Non-Existent Events

The idea of ancestral migration is people migrating from the old world to the new world. And you know birds migrate all the time so I thought I would explore that imagery. The main figure is sort of a pelican, the wings are real pheasant wings. The feet are old shoe trees, probably belonging to a child, the way they're splayed out reminded me of birds' feet. On the back of this figure is this one character just hanging on. You know on any voyage there is always one character who misses the boat or almost misses the boat, so that is why I have this character clinging on to the back.

Ancestral Migration

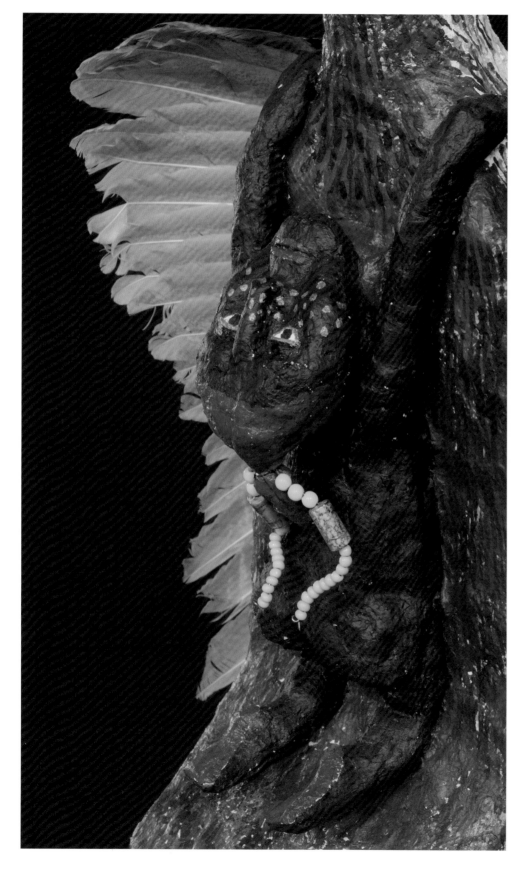

So here I'm talking about the idea of the cowgirl and cowboy. The cowgirl was actually part of my "Saints and Angels" series. When I was creating this work my subject was cowboys but I also had to do a cowgirl. When we talk about westerns you always think about cowboys but we forget that the women themselves also have a large part to play in the life. She is standing on wild roses, wearing an angel and wings on her cowboy hat. I call this **Season of Renewal** because of the calf she is holding – she is looking after it because otherwise it probably wouldn't survive. Now the cowboy, he is **Tall Prairie Grass Racer**. He was one of a series where cowboys control their horses and I thought I would put the point across that the cowboy wants to be in charge. So he is the big figure and he is standing still whereas the horse is the action figure and is much smaller but obviously the cowboy has control of his horse.

Season of Renewal;
Tall Prairie Grass Racer

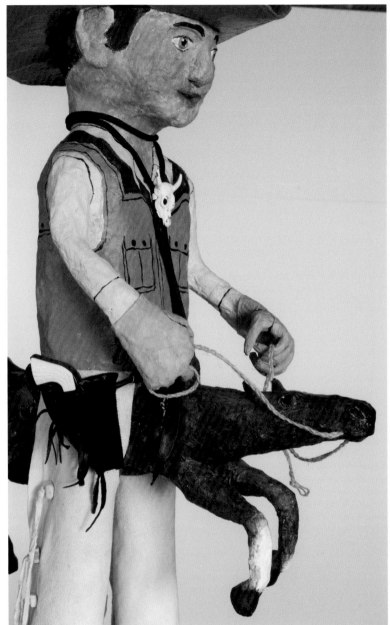

When I created this I was thinking of pollution and what we were doing to the environment and we have to deal with what we have left. Now there's a conflict with people – some people think that there is no pollution whereas others think the world is in a terrible state. So when I was creating the bather it's like she is emerging from a pond but her body is black because of these pollutants. She's come up out of the pond and she's thinking of the days when she was a child, the water was clean and things were probably simpler. She's wringing all of this mud and that out of her hair but she's still surrounded with her stuff because people want stuff. She's got all these embellishments on her because we still want our possessions and we're not willing to give them up. So it's a balancing act – do you want all of this or do you want to have less but maybe a better environment?

The Bather Emerges from the Tailings Pond While Dreaming of the Days When Water was Clean and Sweet-Smelling

This is part of an exhibition I called "Love Follies". It was about people falling in love. All the things that can happen and they don't care because they just love this person. So these are the seven steps you take up to the edge of disaster and finally you fall in. You kind of drown but you don't mind.

7 Steps Before the Plunge of No Return

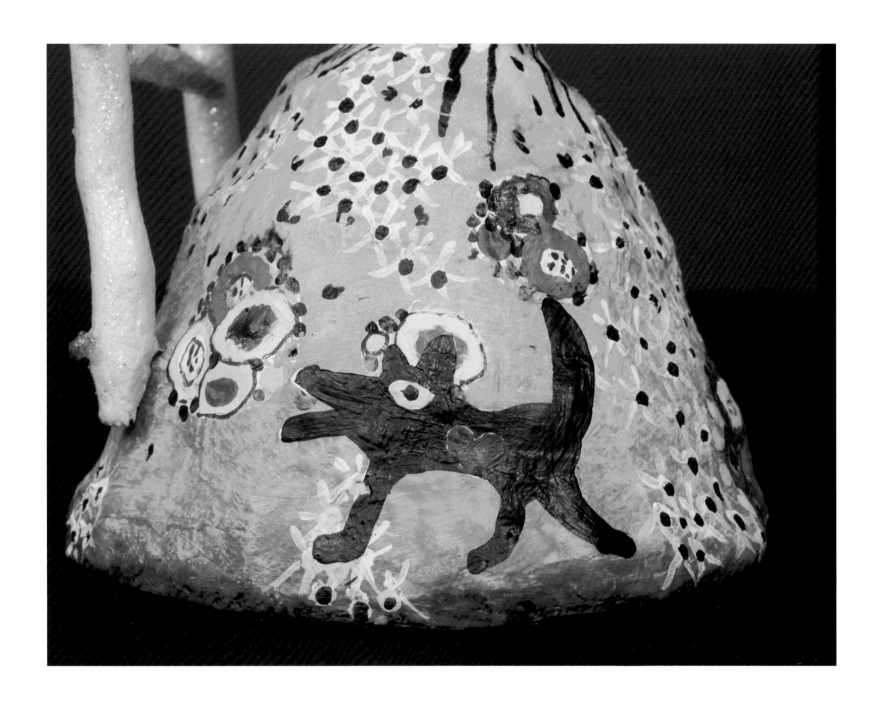

When I created this piece, I was just playing with figures, how to present them. Some people say the piece reminds them of Gustave Klimt, which is interesting, because I really like his work. I also like the Egyptian style, so the woman is sort of Egyptian, she has Egyptian eyes. There is no special story. "Sheba" in the piece is not the woman – she's the cat.

Sheba

Altered Ego 2 resulted from a collaboration between Decidedly Jazz Danceworks and the Alberta Society of Artists. The artists viewed dress rehearsals of a performance called "Pulse" as a source of inspiration and then we would create the pieces. Actually this was a lot of fun because you go to dress rehearsal and you see the dancers perform and you see the dances evolve. One of the performances involved people transforming into animals and the idea was they would take off their skin. The skin would be a coat or sometimes a cape but it's the idea of taking off your skin to become something else – and so this is why I called this one *Altered Ego*. One of the dancers became a deer figure so this is where I got the idea. The red hands dangling from the ears, that was the earrings but the idea is when you pull the skin off and the body will be red.

Altered Ego 2

*This one I call **Moondonna II**. I sold **Moondonna I** so now this is **Moondonna II**. She has this halo around her head studded with stars. Her face is the moon mask and the rest of her head, she's got these little metal gold stars. I used the turquoise beads and the bells to embellish her face. The figure itself, the body, is made from a wasp's nest. The reason I used a wasp's nest as my medium is that I wanted to give it a look where, you know, when you look at the sky at night sometimes you see streaks, like veins, where it's not like a solid colour, and the wasp's nest reflects that beautifully. And then naturally she's standing in my orchid collection which is an added element because you know you have moonlight and orchids and all that stuff.*

Moondonna II

In the late 1970s the Whyte Museum of the Canadian Rockies began a series of exhibitions about the "Exceptional Pass". This is a mystical place full of wonderful things, magical happenings, a legendary place. Apparently it exists somewhere in the Rocky Mountains. For the 1991 show, "Return to Exceptional Pass", I created a boat piece, **The Incredible Return of the Spirit Clans Down the Mystical Waters of Exceptional Pass in their Magnificent Canoe.** This was a very big event so I had dignitaries and very important people in the boat representing their place in the Exceptional Pass. These people are Coyote (free spirit), Yeti (oral tradition keeper), Deer (guardian), Bear (old man of the forest), Cat (reincarnation spirit), Beaver (island builder), Raven (before the transformation) and Mosquito (transformed from the ashes of creative fire).

The Incredible Return of the Spirit Clans Down the Mystical Waters of Exceptional Pass in their Magnificent Canoe

I think it looks Egyptian, so it was inspired by some Egyptian themes. I like the idea of using black and gold, I like the idea of a cat and its progeny resting on her forearm. It's a benevolent cat. That's really all there is to tell. It's a cat.

Mau; Mau, Mau: Mau!

The Logical Nature of Any Voyage is Determined by
the Limits of Interpretation to the Logical Outcome
from the Point of Uncertainty

*That's a mouthful, yes. The idea behind this boat — have you ever gone on
a voyage and you have four or five people and every one has a different
idea of how to get there or how many stops you are going to make or even
what the destination is, and everything is always changing, everyone
is always arguing. The people are like birds, always chattering, always
arguing, you want to go here, you want to go there. They're even different
types of birds, so I gave them different beaks, some are sharp, some are
round like puffins. With all these people telling you what to do you can't
make up your mind. All these people just trying to tell you what to do.
The person in charge, the golden figure, he's just hanging in there trying
to figure things out.*

Ritual for the Search of the Inner Passage

Now here I was having a lot of fun just playing with the idea of an inner passage. The boat is a fish, so maybe the fish is looking for its passage. The helpers are three cats resting on its back. When you think of the inner passage you think of the rib cage, so I painted skeletons on the cats, and they're wearing masks, I just like the idea of masks. They're all motioning forward, maybe they're looking for an inner passage of their own.

This was a commissioned piece for a friend, Georgette, who wanted a portrait of her family. Georgette teaches drama, so I tried to give her some drama, and colour. She is the helmsman of the boat, the matriarch. The figures in the boat are her children. I decided to portray them using the Chinese calendar. Depending on their year of birth, this is the kind of animal they would be. Her son and his wife are dragons, her older daughter is a snake and her son-in-law is a tiger. Her youngest daughter is also a tiger. Her ex-husband, she wanted him included as well, so I showed him as a mask, he was born in the year of the horse, so it's a horse mask. When I created the boat there were just the adults, but a granddaughter came along, so we had to add her, she was a rat. We had a ceremony, with paparazzi and champagne, adding her animal to the boat. This was a first for me. I've never added to a sold sculpture. Usually the owner picks it up and I never see it again. So this was quite different.

Odyssey: Flowing with One's Innate Sense of Direction, Life's Stage Moves on While the Actors Wait for their Cue

Following page: Detail

This figure I made in 2005 as part of a travelling exhibition of the Alberta Society of Artists. The theme of the show was why artists do the things that they do. When I created this piece I wanted to show that the important thing for the artist is to balance the eye, the heart and the hand and hopefully not get the mind to start changing things or interpreting, because the one thing that I've learned is the mind tells you this is what you see and this is how you interpret it. It may not necessarily be true. So this one I call **Balancing the Eye, Heart, Hand.** The show this was in was travelling for two or three years. The Alberta Society of Artists has a lot of travelling shows, and this is actually a balancing act in itself.

Balancing the Eye, Heart, Hand

Ritual in White

This is a winter ritual, celebrating a quiet time, almost hibernation, but there is still enough light to see shadows. The sun is coming, you should make preparations. This is a time of hope, with dances and performances. The mask is part of the ritual, I wanted to make the figure tall so it would have presence. And of course a mask needs eyes. This is what the wire mesh is for. Its amazing how you start out with the one idea and things evolve and change and metamorphosize into something different. Time was also a factor in changes in this sculpture. The hopsacking, for instance, was white, the colour of the mask, but air pollution turned it yellow, which made the knots stand out, they don't blend in now, which changes the character of the piece. But I think I like it this way.

This is part of my "Madonna" series. So the idea is that this madonna is a madonna of the ocean. I know the Inuit have the sedna figure which is a mermaid but this one I thought would be more appropriate as the **Meredonna**. *Sometime down the road I'm going to have to make a Maddonna and a Moodonna and a Meowdonna. So it's the idea of a play on the word "madonna".*

Meredonna

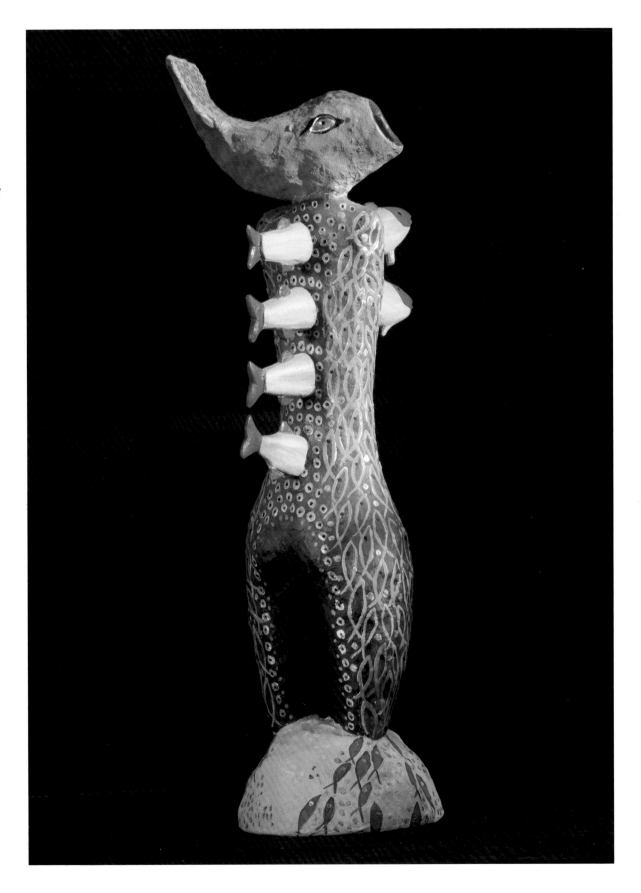

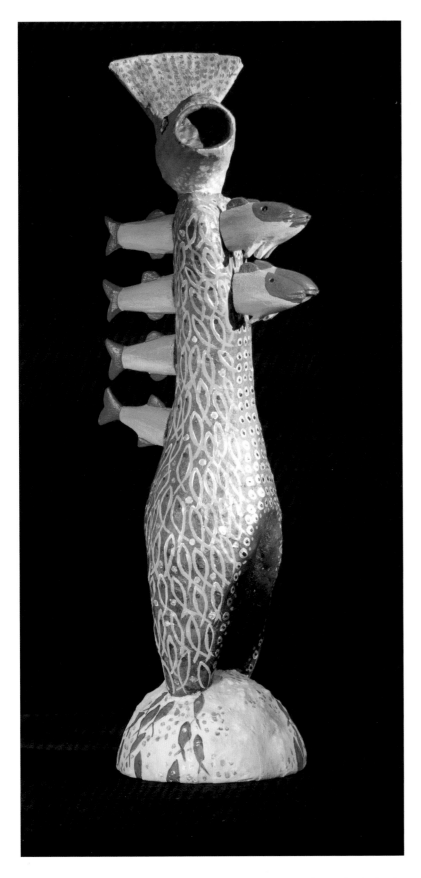

This is **Muddonna**. In the beginning God made Adam and Eve and He used mud. So this is my **Muddonna** and she has a little mudchild. Mud, of course, has to be shown dark. When I paint my sculptures I never use a solid colour without using another to enhance it. Like if there's black I will add blue or red or purple to it so it doesn't read flat. Very often that's a problem with photographing my sculptures – they show up flat looking. That's the reason why I wanted to show the piece with the shadows at the back, to give the figure extra dimension.

Muddonna

Followers to the Edge of the Shock Front

This boat is the container and it's holding all of these people and it's taking them over water to a new existence. The people are really worried. A lot of these people are not happy about going on this voyage. This boat is actually like a guardian figure because she's female and she's protecting these smaller figures. At some point when they come close to land you see these birds and they are ready to fly, they are looking for land. Basically this is the story line about this.

Everyone has guardian figures. You have guardian angels and you have these different monuments or the Chinese have these guard dogs in the temple. I think you should have guardian figures for the house in areas where danger could be lurking even though you don't expect it. So I thought this cat will be the guardian that lives under the stairs. It protects the people who live in the house and it lives under the stairs so that if anything is lurking there it will make fast work of it. Also it's got a snake's tail because it's a guardian figure too and sometimes the cat can sleep and the snake will be wide awake so it's always ready, it's ready to pounce.

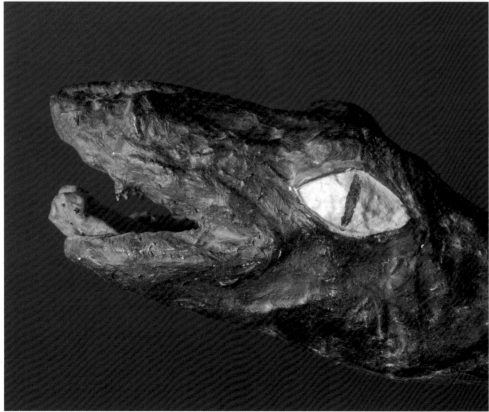

The Cat Who Imagines Himself a Dragon

This too is a guardian figure, looking after people who are in their home. He is wise, someone you can't fool. He has his own ideas, so if anything isn't true the figure will see through it. The idea of the guardian is found in almost every culture. You have charms and amulets to keep you safe in case someone casts a spell when you're sleeping or preoccupied. You need something to keep you safe. That's important to everybody. I liked the shape, so I kept it simple, but I wanted the two bands with the coins to give it a regal look. We've had some discussions whether this is a malevolent or a benevolent figure. Some people interpret the red eyes and the red beak as threatening – and I suppose from some perspectives he may look fierce. But really this is more like a grandfather figure. This is a shamanic piece, a figure that anthropomorphizes animals so you don't know if it's a human or an animal. An ordinary person is made to look extraordinary.

The Sentinel

Immaculate Obsession

*I think originally I wanted to call this piece Immaculate Conception but it ended up as **Immaculate Obsession**. This came about after I was invited to participate in an erotic art show. A few of the women there were lesbians, and some wanted children, so they would go through all these plans to have a child, but they didn't want a man in their life. So that was the idea for the sculpture. I have her holding a dildo – it's an immaculate conception. When the baby is being born you see this halo. In this photograph the graffiti in the background create a sort of ironic contrast with the "immaculate" theme. When I look at this piece, just see it out of the corner of my eye, I think, this has to be India or maybe Africa, it does not have the look that it's in Calgary. Anyway, when I put the piece in the show I told the curator, "If this is too much then I don't mind if you take it down." They didn't mind, and the piece was quite a hit.*

This is one of the pieces that was used in a series of dance performances called "Soul Catchers". If you go by Northwest Coast tradition some people believe that when you're asleep your soul can leave your body and if somebody has evil intent they will steal your soul, or if the soul is lost you put the soul catcher on your chest and it will come back. I thought with the idea of a soul catcher you need a hand and I didn't just want a bare hand so I made one which was the sun and one was the moon and another was the earth and the fourth was water. The dancers carried the hands as part of the Soul Catcher performance. They were the personal guardians of your soul.

Hand Spirit

In a prairie Indian story the great earth goddess makes this huge cookie and when it's done she throws it up in the sky and it becomes the moon. Coyote wakes at night and he nibbles at the moon and keeps nibbling and nibbling until the moon is all gone and then the great goddess looks and there is nothing to light up the night sky so she makes another moon and she throws it up and the coyote comes and he nibbles at the moon again. Now I don't know how accurately the sculpture shows the original legend but I thought I could work with it so I created this piece. The mask on the coyote's chest represents the moon, the full moon, and coyote is getting ready to nibble it. The four arms are to hang on to the moon. It's a very big moon. The decoration on the legs, the squares I painted on them, that's strictly my interpretation of what the prairie's like when you're looking from an airplane. I'm always taken by how much our prairie looks like a quilt where everything is squared off. The eyes are these blue sacred beads from Greece. People wear them because they're supposed to ward off the evil eye and they are supposed to be magical. I love that colour, the cerulean blue. The empty spaces so you can see through the eyes are intended to create the feeling of a mask. Because this is a celestial coyote.

Coyote the Moon Nibbler

Endnotes

1   Throughout this text I have used much information gleaned from numerous meetings and conversations with Pat Strakowski spanning the period from the spring of 2006 to the winter of 2008. In this case Strakowski's memories of the Bridgeland-Riverside district of her childhood are supported by those of Bill Benner in "Growing Up in Bridgeland: The World War II Years", *Heritage Connexions: Newsletter of the American Historical Society of Germans from Russia, Calgary Chapter*, 10/4 (Dec 2002).

2   Pat Strakowski, in *Return to Exceptional Pass* (Banff: Whyte Museum of the Canadian Rockies, 1992), 4.

3   Pat Strakowski, in *The Myth of Exceptional Pass* (Banff: Whyte Museum of the Canadian Rockies, 1985), 33.

4   The series began in 1978 with *Beyond Exceptional Pass*. The second was *Exceptional Pass: The Quests, The Expeditions, The Explorations* in 1982. The third was *Myth of Exceptional Pass* in 1985, and the last was *Return to Exceptional Pass* in 1992.

5   Ed Cavell citing Jon Whyte, 9 Nov 07. Jon Whyte, late poet and historian of the Canadian Rockies, was central in developing the creative rationale for the first show. Ed Cavell was curator of photography at the Whyte Museum of the Canadian Rockies at this time.

6   Aldona Jonaitis, *Art of the Northern Tlingit* (Seattle: University of Washington Press, 1989), 63.

7   Ibid., 64.

8   Ibid., 65.

9   Ibid., 65.

10   Margaret Laurence, "Where the World Began", *A Passion for Identity: An Introduction to Canadian Studies*, Ed. David Taras, Beverly Jean Rasporich, and Eli Mandel (Scarborough, ON: Nelson Canada, 1993), 333-4.

11   Mark Walton, with Pat Strakowski and Kirsten Abrahamson (interviews), "Death Stalks the Muttart Art Gallery", *Artichoke*, 6/3 (Fall/Winter 1994), 35.

12   Ibid., 38.

13   Joseph Campbell and Bill Moyers (interviews), *The Power of Myth* (New York: Doubleday, 1988), 5.

14   Ibid., 6.

15   Roland Barthes, "Myth Today," in *A Barthes Reader*, Ed. Susan Sontag (New York: Hill and Wang, 1991), 93.

16   Kaja Silverman, "From Sign to Subject, A Short History," in *The Subject of Semiotics* (New York: Oxford University Press, 1983), 29.

17   Barthes, 115.

18   Ibid., 115.

19   Ibid., 117.

20   Silverman has described this as, "the signified is endlessly commutable;… one signified always gives way to another, functions in turn as a signifier," 38.

21   Jeff Collins and Bill Mayblin, *Derrida for Beginners*, Ed. Richard Appignanesi (Cambridge: Icon Books, 1996), 16.

22   For instance see Henry Glassie, *The Spirit of Folk Art: The Girard Collection at the Museum of International Folk Art* (New York: Harry N. Abrams, 1989), 88.

23   Michael D. Hall, "American Sculpture on the Culture Möbius," in *Stereoscopic Perspectives: Reflections on American Fine and Folk Art*, Contemporary American Art Critics; no. 11, Ed. Donald Kuspit (Ann Arbor: UMI Research Press, 1988), 13.

24   Donald Kuspit in "Preface" to Hall, xvii.

Acknowledgements

The author, photographer and publisher wish to express their appreciation for the invaluable contribution made by innumerable persons and organizations in the publishing of this book.

- Alberta Crafts Council, especially Joanne Hamel, for assistance in photographing *Dwarf Prairie Shorthorn*.

- Alberta Foundation of the Arts, especially Rowena Lunn, Gwyneth MacPherson and Pat Matheson, for assistance in photographing *Ancestral Migration, Ancestor 12, Converging to the Point of Most Familiar Origin, Dwarf Prairie 10 Prong, Mau; Mau, Mau: Mau!, Memory Shell – Renewal of the Great Cycle, Sheba,* and *7 Steps before the Plunge of No Return*.

- And again to the Alberta Foundation for the Arts, for a grant to support the research and writing of this book.

- City of Calgary, especially Barb Greendale and Rachael Seupersad, for assistance in photographing *Ritual for the Search of the Inner Passage*.

- Greg Clarke of Dallas, Texas for photographing *The Logical Nature of Any Voyage is Determined by the Limits of Interpretation to the Logical Outcome from the Point of Uncertainty*.

- Glenbow Museum, especially Steve Waite, for photographing *The Cohorts*.

- Imperial Oil Limited, especially Al Charlton and Kathryn Davies, for assistance in photographing *The Provider* and *Spider Walk*.

- Ed Cavell, for sharing his recollections about the genesis of the *Exceptional Pass* series of exhibitions at the Whyte Museum of the Canadian Rockies.

- Carol Sheehan, for numerous stimulating ideas that contributed to the writing of the book, including suggestions for various research sources.

- The Whyte Museum of the Canadian Rockies, especially Michale Lang, for providing their archival photograph of *The Incredible Return of the Spirit Clans Down the Mystical Waters of Exceptional Pass in Their Magnificent Canoe*.

In addition, many private collectors who preferred to remain anonymous provided essential assistance by letting us photograph Strakowski sculptures in their collection and sharing with us their enthusiasm for her work.

The Pieces

All sculptures are papier-mâché constructed over a wire mesh armature with wooden base and finished with acrylic paint; some pieces are embellished with found objects. The historical photographs on pages 9 to 14 are courtesy of Pat Strakowsky; all other photographs are by John W. Heintz unless specifically noted otherwise in the list below.

7 Steps Before the Plunge of No Return
Pages 94-95
Height: 44.5 cm (17.5 inches)
Date: 1995
Collection: Alberta Foundation
    for the Arts

About Angels, Flights of Imagination, and Other Grey Areas
Page 28
Height: 65 cm (25½ inches)
Date: 2006
Private collection

Altered Ego 2
Page 100
Height: 43 cm (17 inches)
Date: 2007
Private collection

Ancestor 12
Pages 30-31
Height: 51 cm (20 inches)
Date: 1982
Collection: Alberta Foundation
    for the Arts

Ancestral Migration
Pages 88-89
Height: 101cm (40 inches)
Date: 1985
Collection: Alberta Foundation
    for the Arts

Balancing the Eye, Heart, Hand
Page 111
Height: 37 cm (14.5 inches)
Date: 2005
Collection of the artist

The Bather Emerges from the Tailings Pond While Dreaming of the Days When Water was Clean and Sweet-Smelling
Pages 92-93
Height: 63.5 cm (25 inches)
Date: 2009
Collection of the artist

Beaver Women
Pages 48-49
Height: 27cm to 30 cm (10½ inches to 12 inches)
Date: 1985-86
Collection of the artist

The Cat Who Imagines Himself a Dragon
Pages 120-121
Height: 56 cm (22 inches)
Date: 1986
Collection of the artist

The Cohorts
Pages 78-79
Length: 66 cm (26 inches)
Date: 1989
Collection of Glenbow Museum;
    gift of Douglas MacLean and
    M.B. Laviolette, 2001
Photo: Glenbow Museum

Converging to the Point of Most Familiar Origin
Pages 50-51
Height: 81 cm (32 inches)
Date: 1989
Collection: Alberta Foundation
    for the Arts

Coyote the Moon Nibbler
Pages 126-127
Height: 114 cm (45 inches)
Date: 1992
Collection of the artist

Deformed Angel I
Pages 36-37
Height: 63.5 cm (26 inches)
Date: 2002
Collection of the artist

Deformed Angel II
Pages 44, 46
Height: 66 cm (26 inches)
Date: 2004
Collection of the artist

Deformed Angel 3
Pages 38-39
Height: 90 cm (35 inches)
Date: 2002
Collection of the artist

Dwarf Prairie Shorthorn
Page 52
Height: 25cm (10 inches)
Date: 1985
From the collection of The Alberta
    Craft Council

Dwarf Prairie 10 Prong
Page 53
Height: 46 cm (18 inches)
Date: 1985-86
Collection: Alberta Foundation
    for the Arts

Earth Pauses, Moon Passes
Page 80
Height: 71 cm (28 inches)
Date: 2000
Collection of the artist

Eclectic Visionary
Pages 40-43
Height: 85 cm (33½ inches)
Date: 1998
Collection of the artist

Enchantment Leads to That Which Delights the Eye
Pages 87, 84-85
Height: 61 cm (24 inches)
Date: 2001
Collection of the artist

Every Day is a Good Day When You're Above Ground
Pages 81-82
Height: 56 cm (22 inches)
Date: 1999
Collection of the artist

Followers to the Edge of the Shock Front
Pages 118-119
Height: 74 cm (29 inches)
Date: 1988
Private collection

Ginger
Page 35
Height: 34 cm (13½ inches)
Date: 1988
Private collection

Grandmaster's Hat for Non-Existent Events
Pages 86-87
Height: 30.5 cm (12 inches)
Date: 2007
Collection of the artist

Hand Spirit
Page 125
Height: 94 cm (37 inches)
Date: circa 1988
Collection of the artist

Harvest Moon
Pages 60-61
Height: 71 cm (28 inches)
Date: 2004
Collection of the artist

Identity Protected by Memory Beads
Pages 74-76
Height: 62 cm (24½ inches)
Date: 2006
Collection of the artist

Immaculate Obsession
Page 124
Height: 49.5 cm (19½ inches)
Date: 2000
Collection of the artist

In Collaboration
Pages 54-56
Height: 101 cm (40 inches)
Date: 1990
Collection of the artist

**The Incredible Return of the
Spirit Clans Down the Mystical
Waters of Exceptional Pass in
their Magnificent Canoe**
Pages 102-103
Length: 130 cm (51 inches)
Date: 1991
Private collection
Photo: The Whyte Museum
  of the Canadian Rockies

**Into the Uncharted Bottomless
Go the Brave Company, Secure in
their Flame's Vision**
Pages 32-35
Length: 104 cm (41 inches)
Date: 1994
Collection: Frontenac House Ltd.

Lady in Black
Page 57
Height: 74 cm (29 inches)
Date: 1998
Collection of the artist

Lilith: Third Transformation
Pages 44-45
Height: 66 cm (26 inches)
Date: 2004
Collection of the artist

**The Logical Nature of Any Voyage
is Determined by the Limits of
Interpretation to the Logical Outcome
from the Point of Uncertainty**
Page 105
Length: 51 cm (20 inches)
Date: 1998
Private collection
Photo: Greg Clarke

Mandonna
Page 77
Height: 61 cm (24 inches)
Date: 2005
Collection of the artist

Mau; Mau, Mau: Mau!
Page 104
Height: 61 cm (24 inches)
Date: 1986
Collection: Alberta Foundation
  for the Arts

**Memory Shell - Renewal of the
Great Cycle**
Pages 48-59
Height: 35.5 cm (14 inches)
Date: 1995
Collection: Alberta Foundation
  for the Arts

Meredonna
Pages 114-115
Height: 40.5 cm (16 inches)
Date: 2000
Collection of the artist

Momdonna II
Pages 81-83
Height: 48 cm (19 inches)
Date: 2006
Private collection

Moondonna II
Page 101
Height: 48 cm (19 inches)
Date: 2006
Private collection

Muddonna
Pages 116-117
Height: 45.5 cm (18 inches)
Date: 1991
Collection of the artist

**Odyssey: Flowing with One's Innate
Sense of Direction, Life's Stage Moves
On While the Actors Wait for their Cue**
Pages 108-110
Length: 915 cm (36 inches)
Date: 2007, modified 2009
Private collection

The Provider
Page 29
Height: 61 cm (24 inches)
Date: 1990
Collection of Imperial Oil Limited

**Ritual for the Search of the Inner
Passage**
Pages 106-107
Height: 61 cm (24 inches)
Date: 1989
City of Calgary Civic Art Collection

Ritual in White
Pages 112-113
Height: 165 cm (65 inches)
Date: 1992
Collection of the artist

Saint Luna of the Night Light
Pages 66-67
Height: 112 cm (44 inches)
Date: 1999
Collection of the artist

Season of Renewal
Pages 90-91
66 cm (26 inches)
Date: 1998
Collection of the artist

Sedna's Fashion Statement
Pages 72-73
Length: 30.5 cm (12 inches)
Date: 2009
Collection of the artist

The Sentinel
Pages 122-123
Height: 79 cm (31 inches)
Date: 2001
Private collection

Sheba
Pages 96-99
Height: 51 cm (20 inches)
Date: 1988
Collection: Alberta Foundation
  for the Arts

Spider Walk
Pages 68-69
Height: 122 cm (48 inches)
Date: 1985
Collection of Imperial Oil Limited

Spirit Guide
Pages 62-63
Height: 51 cm (20 inches)
Date: 1983
Private collection

Spirit Guides in their Magic Craft
Pages 70-71
Height: 30.5 cm (12 inches)
Date: 1985
Private collection

Spring Ritual
Pages 64-65
Height: 84 cm (33 inches)
Date: 1985
Collection of the artist

Tall Prairie Grass Racer
Pages 90-91
Height: 72.5 cm (28.5 inches)
Date: 2005
Collection of the artist

**Wisdom Comes from Seeing the World
from a Different Point of View**
Pages 44-47
Height: 73.5 cm (29 inches)
Date: 2005
Collection of the artist

Index